BIG RIG

COMIC TALES FROM A

BIG RIG

COMIC TALES FROM A
LONG HAUL TRUCKER

DON MCTAVISH

NEWEST PRESS

LONE PINE 🌲 PUBLISHING

National Library of Canada Cataloguing in Publication Data

McTavish, Don, 1942-

Big rig

ISBN 1-896300-54-5

1.Truck driving—Humor. 2. McTavish, Don, 1942- 3. Truck drivers—Canada—Biography. I. Title.

HD8039.M795M32 2001   388.3'24'092   C2001-910793-5

Editor for the press: Don Kerr
Cover photo: Tamara Eder
Author photo: Sherwood Studios
Interior design: Erin Creasey

THE CANADA COUNCIL | LE CONSEIL DES ARTS
FOR THE ARTS | DU CANADA
SINCE 1957 | DEPUIS 1957

Canadian Patrimoine
Heritage canadien

NeWest Press acknowledges the support of the Canada Council for the Arts and The Alberta Foundation for the Arts for our publishing program. We also acknowledge the financial support of the Government of Canada through the Book Publishing Industry Development Program (BPIDP) for our publishing activities.

This edition first published by NeWest Press and Lone Pine Publishing

NeWest Press
201-8540-109 Street
Edmonton, Alberta   T6G 1E6
t: (780) 432-9427
f: (780) 433-3179
www.newestpress.com

Lone Pine Publishing
10145-81 Avenue
Edmonton, Alberta   T6E 1W9
t: (780) 433-9333
f: (780) 433-9646
www.lonepinepublishing.com

3   4   5   05   04

PRINTED AND BOUND IN CANADA

This book is dedicated to truckers everywhere, no matter how many wheels are under them or what they haul.

The drivers in my stories get a special thanks.

Acknowledgements

Without a doubt, this book would never have been completed without the assistance and guidance of my wife, Margaret Nelson. She was the one who first recognized the entertainment value of my old memories and insisted on recording them. Her expertise with written English and her blind faith in my story-telling ability have made this book a reality.

My family also deserves a huge thanks for their encouragement.

Rolf Lockwood, editor of the truckers' trade magazine *Highway Star*, really made this book possible. He was the first to read and publish my attempts at humour and continues to publish my stories, some of which appear in this book. Thanks Rolf!

—Don McTavish

Table of Contents

PART ONE

IN THE BEGINNING

Hey, Rookie!

NEW GUY, GRINGO, "hey you," trainee, kid.

Those monikers probably cause a little squirming for a lot of you folks, but in my humble opinion—which is worth about five cents in Canadian funds—we all fell into that category once in our lives. The fact is that not one of us gear crunchers was born with our pudgy little fingers gripping a steering wheel. Granted, some of us caught the scent of diesel at a pretty early age, and our careers were a foregone conclusion.

I still remember the look of horror on my parents' faces when I told them I was quitting high school and pursuing a truck driving job. I think they had me pegged for a doctor, an astronaut or something that paid better than trucking, but my mind was made up. It was their fault anyway because my old dad was a trucker for the first few years of my sorry life.

But hold it. I'm babbling. Back to the story.

Any trucker will tell you that making the decision is the easy part. Getting hired is a whole lot more complicated. There are lots of drivers' jobs out there, but that ugly word "experience" always crops up.

That's the kicker.

Take your average citizen who decides to stay in school and ends up with a diploma. He need only flash that to convince an employer he's experienced. Unfortunately, there's no White Line U available to us, eh gang?

There are, of course, many reputable driver trainer schools out there who do a great job teaching steer, gear, safety and what-happens-if-you-push-on-this-thingy or pull-on-that-whatsis, but they can't cover it all. Sooner or later, you'll need to know how much liquid you can pour into a tank, how to stuff a reefer without freezing the tomatoes or how to stock general freight in a high-cube box without biting your nails off to the first knuckle on your way to a government scale.

You're laughing if your brother-in-law has his own rig and loves your sister enough to take a chance on you, but for most of us, it's done the hard way. A bunch of my fellow pavement mashers started with a fly-by-night operator who always came up short on pay day and thought preventative maintenance was some sort of birth control. Nevertheless, it was experience.

Some brave souls tried to hide their lack of experience behind wallets chained to their belts, fuel stains on their cowboy boots and huge piles of baloney. Their conversation would be full of really cool truck stuff, like "split shift" and "double clutch," but most employers could see through that like panty hose over a post.

Another shaky way to join our ranks was to sell the fifty acres and the Massey Ferguson your folks left you, borrow more loot than you could ever hope to pay back, buy a used truck that was older than dirt and sign up with some outfit that was desperate for power. Usually the finance company or the outfit got all your money, but that was experience too.

One tried and true method is to put your dream of a shiny new fire-belching road cruiser on hold and start small, hiring on as a helper in the oil field, in furniture moving or in warehousing, all of which guarantees a driving job sooner or later. Granted, you're going to get dirty and your back will ache, but it's experience.

Some of the humongous outfits with a zillion trucks have solved the problem of inexperienced pavement pilots. The trucks and trailers are all identical and travel only terminal to terminal on predetermined routes, with an army of supervisors. They have satellite tracking, tachometers, computers and armies of inspectors keeping an eye on every move. The driving is strictly pin-to-pin, with sealed trailers. This is a peachy way to get your feet wet, but there's not a whole lot of challenge. Still, it's experience.

I suppose things have changed a bunch, but curl up in your favourite commander air chair and I'll tell you how I went about it.

At the tender age of seventeen, when the legal age for a chauffeur's license in Alberta was eighteen, finding any kind of work with a transport company was tougher than Aunt Patty's pot roast. I picked out a company that appeared to do a little of everything and just hung around for days. A couple of the drivers treated me like I was almost human, but I was usually ignored. About the fourth day of this, a big, rough, angry guy stomped up to me and bellowed as follows.

"If you're just going to f——ing stand there and bug my f——ing drivers, I might as well put you to f——ing work! What the f——ing hell can you do?"

Lordy! It was love at first sight. By the end of the first day, which went well into the night, I had changed flat trailer tires, fueled up trucks and helped pull tarps over a couple of loads. I'd been named "The Kid," and the only person who talked to me was my new-found boss, who heaped more personal abuse on me than I'd taken in my whole life. Still, I thought I was in heaven.

About a week into this slave labour, Screaming Sam stomped up to me again.

"You're going f——ing swampin'!"

He double-times it over to one of the loaded winch trucks, with me right in his dust, and goes nose-to-nose with an equally cranky-looking driver.

"Take The Kid. Teach him to swamp. Anything happens to him, I'll hunt you down."

Oh goody! My teacher walks with his knuckles just barely clearing the ground, and he already hates me, thanks to our fearless leader. Silly me. No sooner were we out of the gate when a big smile appears on old Sparky's kisser. He introduces himself.

"Don't let the old man scare you. He's got a big heart. You've just gotta frown at him. He figures if you're smiling, you're probably stealing from him or getting paid too much."

Well, I learned plenty from Sparky on that trip and all the others which followed through the months to come. The guys were now letting me drive the rigs, and I was getting the best training there was. Would you believe, I lived through a whole year of that crappola?

The day finally came to apply for my chauffeur's license, and with my heart in my throat, I approached Sam to request use of one of his tractors for my driver's test. I still hadn't seen a sign of this heart he was supposed to have.

"F——-ing charity. Always f——-ing charity! Oh, alright—take Unit 13, but be f——-ing careful!"

What the hell was this? Unit 13 was a nearly-brand-new truck.

"Simon, are you sure?"

Well, stone the crows if a big smile doesn't break out on his face.

"You earned it," he said. Then the frown reappeared, and he was gone.

The test was a joke! The written part was a snap, and now the inspector and I were walking to my truck. The inspector stops in his tracks when he sees it.

"You're driving for old Singin' Sam? Truck looks new—the miserable bastard must finally be spending some of his money!"

Well, he jumps in the cab and reams off his truck stories for half an hour. He finally checks off a bunch of stuff on his clip board, then climbs out, waving me to join him.

"What about the test?" I ask.

"You passed, buddy. If old Sam trusts you with a new rig, he's already tested you tougher than I could."

Well, son of a bee, I had finally found that big heart. I flew back to the office, flashed my newly-acquired wings and got my second smile from the old man. He knew darn well that fancy tractor would seal the deal.

You know, minus a couple of seasons in the oil patch that the old man insisted on, and a couple of years hauling logs just out of curiosity, my whole working life was spent with that company. It expanded like crazy and I got to do everything I'd dreamed of. The best part, of course, was high-miling with a fire-belching road cruiser.

Keep the faith, boys. All it takes is a little patience and some give-and-take. Give all your time to the truck and take a ton of abuse!

Good Ol' Even-Up

FOND MEMORIES OF the Alberta oil patch? Yeah, right. For me, that's like pleasant thoughts of a root canal.

The first pictures I conjure up are snow drifts up to my keester all winter and ankle-deep mud the rest of the year. Mind you, for the teenager that I was, on my first trucking job, it was one hell of an experience. Big, rough and noisy. That pretty well describes the trucks that moved the oil rigs—and the guys who drove them. Living for months on end in camps around these rough, tough dudes and their off-road monsters matured me real quick.

You probably picture Alberta to be all flat, like pee on a plate, but believe me, the northwestern parts, where these immense oil drilling rigs worked, consisted of tree-covered, rugged foothills. The trucks and men had to be as brutal as the conditions. Like any big off-road industry, the trucks were designed for the job. Mining has its monster end-dumps, forestry has its huge log trucks, and the oil field has its wild-looking bed trucks, fondly referred to as "sows." These things fascinated me.

The cabs were pretty standard Autocar, Hayes, Sterling, or what-have-you, but from there back they were all oil patch. Chin-high, oversized tires were mounted all the way around, to accommodate the heavy loads and add a little clearance from that axle-eating gumbo. The twenty-five-foot long decks stood six feet off the ground and were built with railroad tracks for crossmembers. They had indestructible headache racks behind the cabs containing the necessary massive cable winches. These sows could winch fifty ton chunks of oil rig onto their backs and roar away like it was nothing. A dozen or so of these and other assorted trucks tearing a drilling rig apart or slapping it back together in a limited space was a real spectacle. It always amazed me that we all got out alive.

Now, one of these bed trucks was a real freak. Some twisted welder figured a forty-foot deck would be handy to haul pipe. Problem was, the drive axles had to be mounted at the very end for regular winch work, so it had the wheel base of a boxcar. Not only was it impossible to manoeuver in tight spots, but it tended to plow itself into the rhubarb on slippery bends. I got to meet the unlucky soul elected to drive this monstrosity when my turn came to winch him out of yet another ditch.

Howard was your usual, garden-variety oil-patch

skinner, standing over six feet tall with a ten-day beard, muddy jeans, and built like a brick phone booth. Added to all this were black, stained teeth and an ill-fitting glass eye that stared straight ahead while the other eye moved. This had earned Howard the nickname "Even-Up." Seems his fellow patchers figured if he only had one eye and one . . . well, rectum, he was pretty well evened up. It sounded a bit crude, but Howard didn't seem to mind.

Howard looked pretty scary, but turned out to be a friendly and mellow guy. He had one social failing though. Annoyingly, he preferred punching your shoulder instead of shaking hands as a greeting. We became good friends while we did our hard time, but I swear the later bursitis problem I developed in my shoulders was from Even-Up punching them every chance he got.

Anyway, the short bed, gas-powered International with single-axle trailer that I drove for Archie B. saw me through two winters, then I was out of the patch like a cheap hat in a high wind.

I landed a driving job with a general freight company in Edmonton and figured I'd gone to heaven. The freight wasn't covered in crude and the pavement they hauled over didn't stick in the wheels. I stayed with them and eventually worked my way up to long haul, team driving cabover Kenworths. Son of a gun, it didn't get any better than this! Still clean at the end of a day, decent pay and no worries about broken winch lines whipping through the back window and through me. Memories of the patch faded and the chances of seeing those old lifers again were slim. Or so I thought.

Nicky, my regular second driver, could have passed for a patcher with his fire-hydrant build and rough appearance. In reality, he was the quiet type and one of my best friends. I guess because of my flimsy physique, he felt I needed looking after, so he elected himself guardian. This was great when heavy lifting was involved and he insisted on doing the lion's share, but it finally got us into a little trouble.

We walked into the Husky truck stop in Cache Creek together late one night, yapping about something and paying no attention to the other people in there. With no warning, a scruffy-looking dude bounded out of a booth we were walking past.

"Hey, you!" he hollered. Then he punched my shoulder. Hard.

Sheesh! In a split second, an equally scruffy Nicky bumped me out of the way, tackled the shoulder thumper with hands around his throat, and they both ended up sprawled on the floor. But you guessed it: staring up at me through one darting eye was Even-Up.

I grabbed Nicky by his shirt and yelled in his ear.

"He's a friend! He's okay!"

The two of them slowly got up, still eyeing each other but a whole lot calmer, waiting for me to say something.

"Nicky, meet Even-Up," I blurted, quickly explaining who was who, apologizing to the restaurant manager, who had showed up planning to throw all three of us out. Calming the situation cost me three suppers, but the bull session while we ate made it all worthwhile. We got to dazzle Nicky with our oil-patch experiences, or maybe we bored him a little. But I loved it. Howard explained that he too had had his fill of the oil field and had taken a long haul job.

After reminiscing a bit, we decided the patch wasn't all bad, but like the old saying goes, "It's a great place to be from."

And oh yeah, I did finally tell old Even-Up to knock it off with the shoulder punching. Too late to cure my bursitis.

Initiation Rites

IN THE SUMMER of 1970, my wife and I moved to Quesnel in the Cariboo region of British Columbia. The town was smack dab in the middle of, and almost completely supported by, the logging industry. There wasn't much call for an old pavement pounder like me, so hauling logs was the only work I was likely to find. I spread the word that I could "gear and steer" but had never hauled sticks. After about three days, my phone rang. A guy named Bill Mayden, who owned four logging trucks, asked if I could start driving right away.

"You bet!" I said. "I'll be in first thing in the morning to fill out the application." This, of course, was the way it was done, back in the big city.

"Forget that," he said. "We'll do this the easy way. I'll meet you at the shop at 4:00 AM. We'll find out real quick if you can handle this, without wasting paper."

I quickly agreed, and got to the shop on time. There was a shake of the hand and a simple introduction, and then Bill pointed to one of the four trucks parked nearby. I climbed into the driver's seat.

Other than the fact that this Kenworth had bush fenders, and the trailer was up on top rather than behind, it resembled the highway trucks I'd driven. It had a 350 Cummins engine, which was a little stronger than the 335 I'd been used to, and an exotic-looking, two-way radio that made CB radios look like a piece of string with two tin cans. I did a quick walkaround and fluid check, but it didn't impress my new boss—he was almost asleep in that passenger seat

Well, away we went, with Bill waking up just long enough to point when we needed to make a turn. We climbed Six Mile Hill, a two-lane, paved road on the outskirts of town, which was peanuts compared to the mountain passes I'd travelled as a high-miler. I relaxed and thought, "This is a piece of cake."

All of a sudden, the pavement ended, and we were on a gravel road with pot holes the size of basements. Brother, I'd never seen such washboard. I slowed down to about fifteen MPH and looked over at Bill. He was doing up his seat belt.

"You better do yours up because we've got forty miles to go, and at this speed, we'll never make it. Once we get airborne, the shock absorbers will do all the work."

"Well, it's your truck," I said. "How fast do you want to go?"

"Just stay between the trees," he said.

By God, he was right. I hit about fifty MPH, and that truck leveled right off. I looked in the mirror, and those drive wheels going crazy, but the cab was like a Cadillac. The guy who owned the highway trucks I'd driven would have passed out if he'd seen this.

"Driver abuse!" he would have screamed.

Bill said, "Watch for the forty-mile sign with the skull and crossbones on it." Then he went back to sleep.

The huge sign finally showed up, and the skull and crossbones was a warning to the hunters that the area was being logged. I thought this was a little extreme until I started up that road.

The sun was just coming up, and so was Bill. He reached up, grabbed the mike of that radio and babbled something about Unit So-and-So being at Mile So-and-So.

Sheesh! The radio went nuts. There were voices calling locations, and other voices, calling other miles. What had I gotten myself into here? All this racket seemed to mean something to Bill because he all of a sudden pointed up the mountain and said, "Drive up there."

Good grief! That trail was straight up! I quickly reached over, flipped the diff lock and flew at the bottom of that hill. Holy smokes, those ruts and roots! If it wasn't for those seat belts, we'd have been thrown through the roof. I started to feel sorry for that poor old truck.

About a mile up this squirrel run, we came into a big clearing. A big, 980 Cat loader and a bunch of skidders were crawling around like ants. Bill pointed to the loader, parked with his forks in the air, and said, "Pull underneath him."

I'd no sooner done what I was told than my trailer disappeared. That big old loader had stuffed a fork into it somewhere and lifted it off.

"Pull ahead," said Bill. My trailer appeared again, and with a little instruction from Bill, it got hooked to the back of the truck.

I was speechless. Nothing had been said; all this just happened. Man! These guys knew what they were doing.

Bill went into a flurry of instruction, pointing and running around.

"This hooks to that. This comes out. This goes in. Stand back."

And Jesus, the wood started to fly. In ten minutes, it was apparently done because Bill looked up at the loader and sliced his throat with one finger.

"Throw the binder," he said to me.

"You mean this piddly piece of cable? How do we tie this load down?"

"What tie?" he said. "It ain't goin' nowhere. Besides, if you do something stupid, I want the logs to leave, not go through the truck. Head for town, and every time you see a mile sign, call your unit number and that mile sign number into the radio. Wake me when you get there."

"Any idea how heavy this is?" I asked.

"Somewhere around 100 thousand pounds gross, if we're lucky."

Oh, lovely, I thought. And we have to get down that chute we climbed to get back on the main road. I started crawling down this logger's idea of a road and very quickly gained speed. The brakes were working fine, but we were just skidding over the boulders and roots. Bill sensed I was nervous.

"Remember, the road is banked at the bottom on purpose. You can hit it flat out. Relax."

He grabbed the radio again and stated, "New boy coming out of Karl's Landing."

We hit the main road at Warp 7, and two other logging trucks had stopped short of this entrance to let me onto the road. I tell you, it was like a big ballet up there. Dangerous as hell, but everybody seemed to know what they were doing.

The only other piece of instruction I got from Bill was, "Take it easy on the corners. We're real top-heavy."

Somehow we made it, and after unloading at the mill, Bill said, "Drive me back to the shop."

Oh, Lord. I thought I had flunked, but as Bill stepped out of the truck, he said, "Do that two more times today and bring the truck back when you're finished. You got the job."

I had absolutely no idea what the hell I was doing, but I faked my way through the day—the longest fourteen hours I'd ever put in.

No Way Out

BACK IN THE olden days, when I was seventeen, one of my first jobs with Northern Industrial Carriers was "gofer" and swamper. One day, one of the more colourful characters, named Eddie, and I were dispatched with a load of steel sucker rods. These thirty-foot rods went down an oil well and were hooked to those huge, horsehead pumps you see in the oil fields.

Eddie and I had old number one, a single-axle GMC with a single-axle trailer. This old truck was equipped with a five-ton winch, and inasmuch as it was only set up as a tractor, it could be converted to a gin-pole truck.

For you greenhorns out there, gin-poles were long, steel pipes, with fittings at both ends roughly fifteen feet long. These fastened to the rear of the tractor, forming a v-shape and turning the tractor into a small crane. Hence the need for a helper to unload the truck. This was me.

We were destined for an oil well site about a hundred miles out of town, west of Devon, Alberta. It was summer, and we didn't have all that far to go, so we didn't bother taking tire chains, food or water. Oil fields were famous for their lack of signs, and you were given only a land location. This could create problems, and it certainly did this day. We got lost and drove around for hours until we found the right road.

By now it was getting dark, and it was starting to rain like hell. We broke over the top of a long, steep hill and slithered down to the well-head we were looking for, in the middle of a large clearing.

Now, roads in the oil fields are not really roads, just trails that a bulldozer has levelled. Heavy equipment uses the road only twice—once in and once out—to drill the well. After that, only small service trucks or half-tons need to get in. So nobody bothers with drainage ditches or gravel.

By the time we had unhooked from the trailer, rigged up the gin-poles, unloaded the crates at the well-head, stripped down and re-hooked the tractor to the empty trailer, that hill we had come down was a river of soup. Eddie took three or four runs at it, but the best he could do was to crawl half-way up and then do a controlled backup.

We'd had nothing to eat or drink for sixteen hours, and we were both soaked from the rain. I must admit, I was scared. We had no communication, as CB's and cell phones weren't invented yet, and field phones were luxuries we couldn't afford. We were all alone here; that well site was the end of the road, and it could be days before the service crew showed up to install the sucker rods.

Good old Eddie wasn't a quitter. He turned the truck around in the clearing by the well-head and tried two or three times to back up the hill. The last try, Eddie pulled back onto the clearing and just sat in the cab, staring out the windshield. I was now convinced we were going to die.

All of a sudden, Eddie looked over at me and said, "Crank down the dollies on the trailer. We're going to unhook."

I figured he'd gone crazy. A tractor by itself had no hope of climbing that hill. It wouldn't be heavy enough to get the traction.

Eddie pulled away from the trailer, drove around and backed up to one side of it. Then he got out, pointed to one part of the trailer.

"Hook the winch line to that. We're going to flip the trailer over."

I still didn't understand why, but Eddie had that stupid grin on his face that indicated he may have solved the problem.

The trailer went over with a crash. I unhooked the winch line. Eddie came around and backed up to the rear of the upside-down trailer. He got out and helped me tie the winch line properly to the deck. Then he winched the trailer up over the fifth wheel of the truck, as far as it would go. The front edge of the trailer was still touching the ground, but we now had the majority of the weight overtop our drive axle. Slowly but surely, up the hill we went.

With a great holler of joy, we broke over the top. We dragged the trailer another mile to the intersection in the road, and then we dropped and righted the trailer. After hooking everything back up again, we flew as fast as those stinking roads would allow to the nearest open coffee shop. We ate three meals in one sitting.

The boss was waiting on our return to the terminal, and to add insult to injury, he accused us of spending the afternoon in a bar! However, we were still wet and stinking, so he finally believed our story.

After that experience, I felt initiated and became part of the crew.

God, how I hated the oil field!

My Big Start

NOT ALL THE fun in life happened while I was gearing and steering. As a matter of fact, I discovered my love of trucks when I was five years old. In 1947, my dear old dad moved us all to Edmonton from Calgary. He had snagged a job with Texaco, driving a tank truck. The no-rider rule was not enforced in those days, so I got to go along with him a lot. It was only a 1940s model KB-8, body-job tanker, but it was the biggest, most beautiful truck I'd ever seen.

This round of pleasure lasted for the better part of four or five years. Alas, the job didn't pay well, and we were forced to live in the basement suite of an old apartment house. Dad got a real job, working in a refinery in Edmonton, so that was the end of his trucking days.

Lucky for me, Dad was also the manager and

maintenance man for the owner of the old apartment house, and one of his duties was to rent out the other suites. One was a single room on the same floor as ours, and one day Dad rented this room to a young woman named Alice. She took a liking to me although I was only nine or ten. I could come and go as I pleased.

Almost immediately, large trucks started appearing around the place at night. Parking was not a problem, as there was a very large back yard in the old joint. Alice had a day job, but even so these trucks would start showing up shortly after supper most nights. Many were rigged to pull trailers and had bunks for long distance hauling. Some even had two drivers.

Other huge trucks with flat decks and winches mounted on them for use in the oil fields also showed up with two drivers. I quickly discovered that if I hung around Alice when these guys showed up, she would arrange for one of the drivers to take me for a ride in the big truck for an hour or so while the other driver "visited." I would get driven around town and taken to truck stops four nights a week or better. It was great, and I learned a lot about trucks into the bargain.

One day, I was thoroughly disgusted to discover Dad had asked Alice to leave. He explained to me, stuttering and stammering, that these men weren't arriving on visits. They were customers. I understood just enough about sex to see where he was coming from. That was the end of a beautiful relationship with Alice and those wonderful drivers.

Fortunately, our old house was right across the lane from a large printing company, and large delivery trucks came and went all day long. I, of course, was attracted to these trucks like flies to a cow pie. One paper supply company in particular, named Barber-Ellis, had a fairly new, five-ton body job, driven by a guy named Lumpy. He was biker type, complete with a chain on his wallet, a leather cap and heavy boots. He had gotten the name Lumpy because he was big-chested and had huge muscles on his arms.

In those days, forklifts and other conveniences were few and far between, so most freight was loaded or unloaded by hand. When Lumpy picked up these huge bundles he was delivering, his T-shirt would get all lumpy from the muscles. He appeared pretty menacing, but I discovered he was a very friendly and gentle guy.

After a week or so of running over every morning when he showed up, I finally got the nerve to ask if I could go along for the ride. I beamed like crazy when he said, "Why not? But," he said, "we better go ask your mom."

Lumpy walked over to the old house with me and, surprisingly, Mom said okay. I guess perverts weren't a big worry in those days, but even if they had been, Mom needn't have worried about Lumpy.

She quickly threw a couple of apples in a bag, and away we went. I spent the rest of the day helping Lumpy and enjoying every minute of it.

Lumpy said I could go along any time I wanted, so four days out of five, I was waiting at 7:00 AM at the printing company, Lumpy's first stop. The first few days, Mom made me a sandwich, but Lumpy always ate at a truck stop, so I would have to sit in the truck alone. By now, I had helped him enough that I could identify the codes on the paper packages and read the packing slips. One day I got a pleasant surprise.

Lumpy said, "You're a good helper, and you need to be paid." So just before lunch, he handed me seventy-five cents.

"Come into the coffee shop with me," he said, "and spend it on lunch."

I can still remember how proud I was to walk in with Lumpy, who seemed to know everybody in the joint. I was prouder still to be introduced as his helper. There wasn't one chuckle or smart crack, and I can only assume it was either because they were scared of Lumpy or they held him in high regard.

I never saved a penny from all this because what Lumpy paid me always just covered the lunch. He needed my help like a nun needs nuts, but I guess he couldn't stand the thought of me sitting outside by myself in the truck, so he invented this way of avoiding the appearance of charity.

I rode around with Lumpy for three summer vacations straight, having the time of my young life. I'll never forget him. What a super dude he was!

PART TWO

COLOURFUL DUDES

Goodbye, Nicky!

We were on our way to Endako, up in northern British Columbia. The roads had been sheer hell for hours, slippery for miles. My partner, Nicky, had been doing most of the driving, but I had just taken over at the Mt. Lemoray truck stop.

When we pulled out, I was following a tanker, and we were both headed for Pine Pass, a steep and winding hill we had to climb. I was already dreading that. I left my backup lights on to watch for spray coming off the tractor tires. No spray, and you're on ice. For miles, me and that tanker were making spray. Good news. But at that time of the night, after midnight, ice could form anytime.

Nicky was sound asleep in the bunk behind me, and he was a good sleeper. Well, we started up the pass, and the tanker was doing fine, so I figured there was no problem. Then, half-way up the hill, the tanker seemed to be pulling away, which shouldn't happen, because I'm loaded light and I know the road as well as the tank driver. I take a glance in my mirror, expecting to see spray, but it's gone. Oops! We're on ice, and I'm spinning my wheels.

We're still moving around thirty MPH, but we've got a long hill to climb yet. By now, the tanker's lights have disappeared, so we have a problem. Probably we'll have to chain up. The trick with that is, it's a two-man job. The driver has to try and keep the rig in a straight line and burn down to pavement, while his partner jumps out and throws a chain over at least one wheel. The rig stays put long enough to put on the rest of the chains. Otherwise, the truck will slide backwards, and there's a wreck. Getting those tire chains on quickly is real important.

With this in mind, I call out, "Nicky, wake up!"

No response.

We're still moving at a pretty good clip, but I figure it can't last, so I call out again.

"Nicky, get up! We got a problem."

I remembered Nicky was a possum, and hated to get out of bed. So I felt sterner measures were necessary. I slowly opened my driver's door.

"Goodbye, Nicky!" I hollered and slammed the door shut.

Nicky bailed out of the bunk like a turd out of a tall horse and dived out the passenger door, still in his shorts. He thought I'd lost it, and the rig was going over the bank.

We were still moving at ten or fifteen MPH, and my first thought was that Nicky might roll under the wheels of the trailer. But as I glanced into the ditch-side mirror, I saw him back on his feet, running up the hill after me, shaking both fists in the air. I had no choice but to keep going and hope I was getting enough traction to make it to the top of the hill, which I could see by now. Nick was going to be no help because he was a long way back—and mad as hell.

I slithered over the crest at a crawl, but I had made it. I pulled off to the side behind the tanker, who was waiting for me. Nicky arrived a minute later, cold, pooped and mighty mad. I'm sure if he had any strength left, he would have killed me. He was one of those no-neck guys, built like a fire hydrant.

I quickly realized he was more excited from fear than from anything else. I explained that I'd had to think of something fast to get him out of the bunk, but that I would never bail out on him. He took a quick look down the hill and realized that if we had spun out like I said we were going to, we would have ended up at the bottom of a 400-foot canyon. So being alive was better. Thank God Nicky loved me; he forgave me and climbed back into the cab.

The tanker driver had walked back to see how we were doing, and I asked him how he had climbed the hill with no problem. He laughed.

"I forgot to mention, when we talked at Mt. Lemoray," he said, "I'm only half loaded. Only my front tanks are full, and so I could climb a wall."

Of course he could climb! All the weight he carried was overtop his drive axles. My load was distributed the full length of my trailer, so I had only half the traction he could muster.

I hated winter driving, especially in northern BC. If God had meant us to truck up here in the winter, she'd have put reindeer under the hood instead of horses.

Red Hot Lover

I take you back to a moment in the early 60s, when I and most of the other drivers that worked for a small company were in our twenties. Eddie, Tiny, and I had just finished loading three truckloads of steel pipe in Edmonton for delivery to an oil-drilling rig near Rocky Mountain House.

I loved working with these two guys, as they were good friends, and they were both pretty unusual characters.

Tiny wasn't tiny at all. He stood six foot, seven inches, and weighed over 350 pounds. Rumour had it that he had a gland problem of some kind and was still growing. Maybe. Needless to say, he was strong as a bull and a very imposing figure.

Eddie, on the other hand, was a pretty common size, but had an ego that wouldn't quit. Man, what a yapper!

Anyway, we finished loading around six o'clock at night, and while we were having supper on the Edmonton outskirts, we decided to continue on to our destination. It was only about a six-hour trip. Normally we would have headed home, then left after midnight, but we were still feeling good, and it made more sense to go then.

Most of these drilling rigs we delivered to were equipped with their own camps, and we could usually get a bunk and a meal. As it turned out, when we arrived around 2:00 AM, we discovered this rig was fairly close to town, so they hadn't erected a camp. The good news was that the rig was working around the clock, and they had extra rig hands, who volunteered to unload us right away. The rig had ordered just a shade over two truckloads of pipe but not enough for a full third load, so we had split the order in three, giving us all light loads. Tiny was the last to unload, and it was agreed Eddie and I would go ahead and we'd meet him at a twenty-four-hour coffee shop in Rocky Mountain House. Tiny would only be twenty minutes behind us anyway.

Eddie and I sat down at a table in the coffee shop, tired and hungry. There were only two other men in there and the waitress. I don't know where he got the energy, but Eddie started chatting up the waitress as soon as she came to take our order. It seemed like a waste of time to me, as she appeared a bit homely and porky, and not worth the effort, but Eddie always felt the need to make a pass at anyone who didn't shave above the neck. This one probably did.

Unfortunately, Eddie was a bit on the homely side too, and he didn't score very much. The yapping didn't seem to be working, so Eddie thought another neat trick would win her over. She had already taken our order and set the bill on our table. Eddie took the bill, set it overtop the glass of water she had served him and flipped the whole works upside down. Well, we all know it will hold water, as long as you don't try to tip it back up again. She was not impressed and told Eddie to quit screwing around.

This attracted the attention of the two gentlemen sitting at the other table. They appeared to be hunters, as they had the usual bright, heavy jackets, boots, and large knives in sheaths hanging off their hips. One of these guys tells Eddie to quit bothering Mable (or whatever the hell her name was). This indicated to me the three of them were all friends and it was time to shut up.

But not good old Eddie. I guess he figured if his baloney and his neat trick hadn't worked, then maybe "macho" would impress her. He tells these guys to take a hike.

I am now frozen in my chair, picturing myself dangling off the end of one of those knives, and nineteen is way too young to die. All of a sudden, the coffee shop door opens and in comes Tiny, stooping over to get through, just in time to see one of these warriors grab Eddie by his jacket. You gotta picture that Tiny is as greasy and disheveled as Eddie and I are from handling that pipe, and he looked pretty scary.

He booms out, "You got trouble, Eddie?" and starts walking over towards us.

The two great, white hunters took one look at him, then at each other, and with silent agreement they let go of Eddie and headed for the kitchen.   Fast.

I can only assume the place had a back door or they were hiding in the fridge, because they never returned.

Well, it seems that Eddie the Red Hot Lover had remembered Tiny was only twenty minutes behind us, and he was timing it pretty close. He knew darn well Tiny wouldn't waste any time because he would be plenty hungry.

We owed Tiny big-time, of course, and offered to buy him breakfast. The waitress looked too nervous to make any more trouble, so she took Tiny's order of six eggs, scrambled, a quart of milk, six slices of toast, and as many potatoes as would fit on the plate. She even stood patiently as Eddie, the Ukrainian Lover, made one last attempt. Unbelievable.

She asked Tiny if he wanted coffee, and he got to use his usual one-liner, "I don't drink the stuff. It stunts my growth." I'm still not sure why I had to pick up half of Tiny's tab, but what the heck, I'm still alive. And we were so wide awake now that we drove all the way back to Edmonton without stopping.

I gotta tell you, that Tiny was one unusual guy. As much as it's not part of the story, here's another Tiny tale. He and I had come in after midnight on another occasion, and as we pulled into the company yard, we witnessed a couple of teenagers climbing out of Tiny's old, 1950s model four-door car. I never saw two kids move so fast.

When we got to the car, it was running, and they could have stolen it because Tiny always left it unlocked with the keys in it. Theft wasn't such a big deal back then. We quickly figured out the little pukes couldn't drive it. You see, Tiny had moved the seat way back, almost touching the rear seat, and he'd lowered it too. Those kids not only couldn't reach the pedals, they couldn't see over the steering wheel. They must have figured the gorilla who owned this car was riding in one of those two trucks pulling into the yard, and they didn't want to mess with that. Smart kids.

That Tiny was a really unusual guy.

The Coffin Box

HERE'S ANOTHER TINY story. This one also involves a really strange truck. The rig was a single-axle conventional Leland tractor that belonged to an owner-operator named Lonesome Len. The rig had an air-cooled diesel engine, so there was a big-mother fan at the front where the rad should be. It had a grill over it, but it looked for all the world like the front end of a jet engine.

Now, we're talking back a bunch of years, so I have no idea what year this rig was, and I haven't seen one like it since, but it must have been a 1950-something. When Lennie fired this sucker up, especially in cold weather, you could hear it for miles. It would bang and clang and scream and smoke, and you'd swear it was going to fly to pieces. Eventually, though, it would smooth out and cut back to a dull roar. Lennie had found a used coffin box sleeper somewhere, revamped it a little, and mounted it on the back of the Leland.

Now, this baby was a true coffin box. There were no end doors in it, like your modern bunk, and the only way in and out was the hole Lennie had cut through the back of the cab and into that box.

The fleet operator that Tiny and I drove for used to hire Lennie on occasion, mostly because they were friends, as leased operation was not a big deal in those days. One of the hauling contracts this company had was with the Alberta Bridge Branch. We would truck bridge components to the four corners of Alberta, up some roads we didn't know existed.

Tiny and I got dispatched on one of these Bridge Branch safaris, along with four other trucks—including old Lonesome from Edmonton—to a site out of Hinton. All the six trucks had pretty piddly power and the highways back then had more curves than the YWCA, so we figured on an eight-hour run.

Well, the trip went a whole lot better than expected, and we arrived at the site about two hours early, in the wee hours of the morning, with Tiny being the last truck in line. For the rest of us, it meant we could just stretch across the seats and get some sleep.

But it wasn't so easy for Tiny. It was still pretty chilly out, and leaving the door open to dangle the extra was out of the question. Lennie was seat-stretcher size, so when Tiny begged to use the bunk, Lennie—soft touch that he was—agreed to it. But it was a Lennie-size opening into the bunk, of course, so it was going to be a real tight squeeze. Tiny took a shot at it anyway, and with a bunch of grunting and groaning, he finally disappeared into the bunk.

The bridge crew arrived with the sun and started unloading the trucks, with Lennie second in line. In order for the trucks to get close enough to the crane to lift off the heavy chunks we all carried, there had been a clear patch bulldozed off to one side for us to turn around, and then we'd back up to the bridge site. This called for the tractor to drive through a dip that had once been the ditch, and when Lennie drove through this dip, the truck swayed from side to side.

Unfortunately, that coffin box—with Tiny still in there—only gave about a half-sway, then leaned to one side and dropped about four inches, gentle as you please. We all ran over to inspect things and discovered the sleeper hadn't ripped loose but had bent the mounts.

Now we had a problem: how to evacuate Tiny?

Turns out Len had cut the same size holes in the cab and bunk, but they no longer lined up and the entrance was four inches smaller than when Tiny had grunted his way inside. No way Tiny was coming outta there!

We other four drivers offered quite a bit of valuable advice, of course, like "drive forward real fast, then brake and he'll shoot right out." Or, "wait till he loses fifty pounds." But neither this nor our rib-aching laughter seemed appreciated. I still laugh when I think about this one.

Fortunately, the problem was solved in short order. After unloading old Lonesome, Lennie got the crane driver to swing his hook overtop of the sleeper, and with the aid of a couple of fabric straps, a gentle tug and a mighty heave from a couple of us on the low side, she popped close enough into place to let Tiny out. Actually, he was out of there in a blur, heading for a bush. Turns out his bladder had been sending him signals all the while.

It seems Lennie had used some pretty rinky-dink metal to mount that thing and because he always ran single, the bunk never had any weight on it when the rig was moving. You can bet Lennie put stronger mounts under it when he got back to town.

Brother! I could sure see where the name "coffin box" came from! If you were ever in one of those when the rig smucked something, you'd have as much chance of surviving as a cat's tail in a room full of rocking chairs.

The Big Shot

YOU JUST NEVER know how the trip will go. So far we'd been lucky. My team driver and I had got our good old cabover Kenworth through the mountains into Vancouver without a scratch. For the middle of December and the lousy road conditions, even that much was amazing.

So we thought we were on a roll. We got a pin-to-pin switch at the Vancouver terminal for a Saskatchewan-bound load. That sure beat the hell out of worming through Vancouver traffic, waiting hours on the water-front, or poking forty-five feet of trailer into a hole meant for body jobs at some nasty, old warehouse.

All ready to go, we split the Vancouver terminal like a pair of cheap slacks and headed east. It was pouring rain when we left, but we knew that wouldn't last long. As any high-miler running the west coast will tell you, the weather changes every mile. With the high peaks and low valleys, the temperature goes up and down like a new bride's pyjamas. As you start to climb, rain turns to black ice and fog, then to blinding snow.

By the time we got into Rogers Pass—God, I'd love to meet Roger and tell him what I think of his stupid road—we were in a major snow storm. The flakes were coming down the size of small pigeons and the "Closed" signs were blinking at the west gate. Oh, lovely! We're in the middle of nowhere, there's no room to turn around, and traffic is almost non-existent. It's only a few days before Christmas.

Well, after sitting there for a couple of hours, wishing I'd taken piano lessons so I could work in a nice, warm bar somewhere, the storm passed. Minutes later, a very large snow plow appeared at the gate. Soon the "Pass Open" sign blinked on and we were gone, trying like crazy to keep up to that plow.

We kissed him goodbye at the summit and ended up in pretty deep snow again. But what the hay! We were headed downhill, the storm had passed, and the full moon shining on all that snow made me forget about piano lessons. Even Field Hill, the last grade we had to climb, posed no problem. Oh, sure, the old girl wiped her feet a couple of times, but up we went.

We were now rolling through Banff National Park in the wee hours of the morning. My partner was asleep in the bunk, and inasmuch as there was still lots of snow, all was going well. The road had been reduced to four ruts: two westbound and two eastbound. It was slippery, but it was still a clear night, and visibility was good.

At that particular moment, we were clinging to a slight downhill grade that stretched for miles. Off in the distance, and obviously off the highway, I could make out some red lights. As I approached, I realized they were the tail lights of a car that had slid about forty feet off the road and lay buried in deep snow. Lucky for the driver, there were no ditches at this point, only flat patches alongside the snowy highway.

I hadn't seen any other traffic for hours, including trucks. So I figured I'd better stop and help this poor, lost soul. I was well past him by the time I rolled to a stop, due to the slippery conditions. I carefully backed up, put on my flashers, and stepped out of the cab into the cold, morning air.

One quick look and I could see the car was a large, expensive Lincoln, buried in snow half-way up its doors. I figured I'd have to chain up in order to pull him out of there. This was a pain in the ass, but I couldn't just leave him there. After all, I was a Good Samaritan. At least we could give him a lift.

It seemed the first thing I'd better do was get a closer look at the car and tie something onto it, so I took a tie-down chain off my headache rack. That chain weighed thirty-five or forty pounds, but I threw it gallantly over my shoulder and marched into the waist-deep snow. With a great deal of falling and swearing—and by following the trail he'd made—I finally arrived at the rear of the Lincoln.

Just as I was catching my breath, the driver's window rolled down, and a calm voice drifted out.

"Be careful of the bumper, kid."

Sheesh! I couldn't believe it. I quickly turned around and stumbled back to my truck, chain and all. This bastard was going to freeze to death or die of carbon monoxide poisoning before another Good Samaritan came along, and yet all he cared about was his bumper!

When I arrived back at the truck, my partner's head was sticking out the bunk curtain. I related the story to him and he gave his thoughtful reply.

"Screw him!" he said. Then he went back to sleep.

Still fuming, I drove to our next truck stop at Valley Gap, about two hours up the road. By the time we arrived, the milk of human kindness had welled up once again, and I called the local RCMP to let them know about the Lincoln. I explained what had happened, and the officer at the other end offered his wise, professional opinion.

"That idiot deserves to die! But we'll look into it."

Well, the rest of the trip was pretty uneventful, but we sure wondered what had become of that big shot. On a return trip to Vancouver after Christmas, we stopped once again at Valley Gap. I called the same RCMP office and was told they had successfully towed out the Lincoln and that our reporting it had probably saved the guy's miserable life.

Don't you just love a happy ending?

Pistol Packin' Partner

OF ALL MY weird-and-wild years of trucking, team driving was the most memorable aspect. The experience of two guys, stuffed in a space roughly the size of a walk-in closet for days or weeks on end, probably wouldn't appeal to Joe Average, but I got a great kick out it. I liked the company during the boring trips and the help when things went haywire. Most of the drivers I got teamed up with were absolute gems, but I got the odd rough stone.

Hey, life is like that.

I must tell you about one of those unforgettable trips. It's a spring day back in the 1960s. I've got trusty old Unit 21, a cabover Kenworth, all hooked up and ready to roll at the Edmonton terminal. This is going to be one of those "jammy" trips because I'm loaded light and headed direct to the Vancouver branch. No squirrel trails or unheard-of destinations this trip.

I've been assigned a team driver named Bill Something-or-Other, newly-hired off the spare board. He seems like a decent sort, but very quiet, and awful uptight. He turns out to be a pretty good driver, staying between the lines and playing the four-and-four trannies like a piano.

So I figured all was well.

Bill drove the first shift, and for the hour or two that I kept him company, he didn't say ten words. So I eventually retired to the bunk. We traded places at a truck stop west of Calgary, and to this point, the trip had been uneventful. The traffic wasn't nearly as heavy in those days, so we were making pretty good time. We were within an hour of our next switch point when Bill climbed out of the bunk and plopped into the jump seat beside me.

I noticed he was carrying a small travel bag. He didn't say "boo," but simply opened the bag and pulled out a big, honking revolver. Now this might not shock your present-day skinner, but back then, a hand gun was something we used for greasing the rig.

Seeing the firearm, I tightened up like an eagle's ass in a power dive. I watched out the corner of my eye as he proceeded to clean the thing with a rag. I kept silent for a few minutes, but finally curiosity got the better of me.

"Uh . . . why are you carrying the cannon?"

I had to ask because there just wasn't any need for artillery. Number one, truck hijackings generally involved booze or cigarettes, which we didn't haul. Number two, we never stopped in one place long enough to cause jealous husbands. And three, road rage shootouts hadn't been invented yet.

In answer to my question, Bill smiled and replied that he had been a policeman for years, back in Ontario, and had had to deal with some pretty nasty people. He said he figured that one of these criminal types might come looking for him some day, so he needed to protect himself. He told me he always insisted on carrying the gun.

I tried to keep my tone level.

"No shit!" I said, picturing some hard-looking guy showing up and blasting big holes in my beloved cabover Kenworth, and me.

I don't want you readers to get me wrong. I had certainly seen guns in my day, but packing them around in the truck was unusual, to say the least. I wasn't worried about Bill being a problem. It was the people seeking him who concerned me a twitch.

Nervous, I pulled into the Husky truck stop at Sicamous, wondering how I should handle the situation. I decided to ask Bill to go ahead and get us a booth while I went to phone in our position. This was company policy.

When the dispatcher came on line, I spoke as calmly as I could.

"What's the idea of hooking me up with Wild Bill

Hickock? This guy is carrying a gun the size of a tree and claims that some criminal types might be looking for him. You don't pay me enough to dodge bullets. What can I do?"

The dispatcher paused a moment. Then he had a brilliant idea.

"If he's not pointing the gun at you, keep going. We'll worry about it when you get to the Coast."

Reluctantly, I agreed and walked into the restaurant.

The ten words I had got from Bill in the truck seemed like jabbering compared to what I got now. All through supper, I asked questions and got nods and grunts in reply. The whole time we sat there, Bill glanced around nervously and pretty soon he had me doing it too. I couldn't wait to exit the joint.

A few minutes later, with Bill behind the wheel and me in the jump seat, we headed west. I tried a short stretch in the bunk, but sleep was just not to be. That little bag of Bill's was down by my feet, ever reminding me at the next stop some bad dude might show up and shoot us both.

We managed one more truck stop in the Fraser Canyon, and it was even worse than the one in Sicamous. By now, we're both tired, and there's a lot more people in this restaurant to keep an eye on. Fully half of them looked like killers to me.

Away we go again, with me behind the wheel. The whole way into Vancouver, I was checking out the other drivers, and every motorist I saw looked like Al Capone to me. I could just picture my miserable life ending before we got there. And sooner or later, I'd have to get some sleep.

As it turns out, the problem sort of solved itself. On arrival at the Vancouver terminal, we were instructed to lay over for lack of east-bound freight. This meant a hotel room and a chance to relax (if that was possible).

Shortly after we checked in to the local "bedbug," Bill grabbed his little bag and said, "I'm going out for awhile. See ya."

I spent the balance of the night with the curtains closed and one wary eye on the door. Next morning, I woke up to discover that Wild Bill hadn't returned. After cleaning up and checking out of the hotel, I hung around the restaurant for a bit, waiting, but there was no sign of Bill.

I headed out to the truck, parked outside in the lot, thinking he may have crashed there, but no go. Finally, I had to go back to the office for new orders. I wondered if they would have heard from him, but they hadn't. I killed as much time as possible, then, to my relief, I was ordered to head east—solo.

I'm told he never even came in to pick up his paycheque.

PART THREE

GOOFY SITUATIONS

Why Me?

I WAS FINALLY headed home after three weeks of moving oil rigs in a place called Virginia Hills. This was part of the Alberta oil-patch, way off in the boonies, out of a town called Whitecourt. It had been a tough three weeks, with lots of snow and it was colder than an Eskimo's nose. It was December, in the winter of 1959, and of course, winters really were worse back then.

My trusty steed at the time was a gas-powered 427, 1957 International bed truck, with a single-axle float. For those of you who were never blessed with work in the oil field, I'd better explain the rig.

These trucks were all equipped with heavy-duty winches and decks about twenty feet long—we called them "beds," hence the word "bed truck." They were designed to self-load and carry heavy drilling-rig components. The float was a flatdeck trailer with no landing legs.

We used the winch to lower and raise this trailer onto its nose. It was designed as a ramp so that large, heavy pieces could be pulled onto the deck by using the winch truck from behind.

Anyway, back to the story. I was on the paved highway, about half-way between Whitecourt and Edmonton, heading east in a blinding snow storm. Luckily, I was empty and the traffic was nil, so all was going pretty well.

As I broke over the crest of a short hill, I thought I could see tail lights through the snow ahead. Because of the storm, they were there and then they were gone again, but I figured I'd slow down, just in case.

Good thing I did, because—sheesh!—there was an old car stopped right in the middle of the road, with its lights on and the engine running. I got stopped just feet short of smacking it in the trunk. I flipped on my flashers and back-up lights, then bailed out of my cab, ready to do battle with the idiot in that clunker.

I looked in the driver's side window and saw two white-knuckled, old ladies, staring straight ahead. There was no way they would have died at the same time, so I figured it might be fear. I rapped on the window, and after what seemed an hour, it cranked down about two inches. Bingo! It was fear all right.

"Lady, you can't park here." I said, with a fair bit of passion in my voice. "You're gonna get killed! I could hardly see you through the snow, and my truck was pretty lit up."

I have to slip another editorial note in here. We in the "patch" did so much work in the dark, that I swear we were part bat. We had the trucks rigged, front and back, with aircraft landing lights. Which meant I could make the road look like the sun was up.

The little, gray-haired driver said, "Sonny, I'm not moving Isabel"—or whatever the hell name it was she gave her car—"another foot. We darned near went off the road a dozen times in this snow, and I'm scared to death."

"Madam," I says, very calmly, "there's a public pull-out about a mile up the road. Drive your car up there and I'll give you a lift into town. I can't just leave you sitting out here because if the traffic don't getcha, the carbon monoxide will."

She seemed to care more for that old, forty-something Ford than she did for her life, because she stated, and very emphatically, "I'm not leaving this car."

By now, I was not only tired, but my back was covered with snow from bending over and begging this old coot to move, so I said, "Drive the car slowly up to the pull-out. I'll go ahead of you. Just follow my lights. When we get there, I'll drop my trailer and load your car onto it."

I couldn't stand the thought of just leaving these two old gals in the middle of nowhere. These, of course, were the days before CB radios or cell phones, so I was on my own.

Well, the old dears finally agreed to this, so after dropping the trailer on its nose, pulling around behind, yarding the winch line down to the car, and gently pulling it on board, we were all set. I shoved the two grannies into the cab, and away we went.

God, what a trip! A hundred miles of hearing what a great guy I was and how come I drive so fast? Good grief! If I'da gone any slower, their car would have passed me!

Finally, after what seemed like days, we arrived at a twenty-four-hour truck stop on Edmonton's outskirts and while my two girlfriends waited in the coffee shop, I unloaded their clunker. By now, I'm soaked, frozen, hungry and real beat.

I sauntered into the coffee shop and whaddya know, the half-dozen people, including the waitress, clapped like hell. Apparently, the ladies had told everyone what I'd done. So I got a free meal out of it, and the ladies offered me twenty dollars, which wasn't small change in those days. By the looks of their clothes and the car they were driving, I figured twenty dollars would have cleaned them out, so I declined. But I got a big kiss from both of them, and that was worth way more than twenty bucks anyway.

I get a warm feeling whenever I think of this episode because those two old girls wouldn't have had a hope if I'd just left them where I'd found them.

Little, White Lie

IT LOOKED AS if a good day was going to turn bad. Unit 16, our usually-dependable, 1960, tandem-axle cabover Kenworth had developed a glitch just before we were ready to leave the Edmonton terminal. The truck was then four years old, so I figured these things could be expected. But the mechanics took a quick look and advised us repairs would take four or five hours. Not good.

Fortunately, I was teamed up as second driver for Dale, one of the old hands, a guy with a great sense of humour. He was always a pleasure to run with.

We'd had our forty-foot, flatdeck trailer loaded fairly quickly at the steel mill nearby, and it was still pretty early in the day. The steel grinding balls we had on were destined for a large mine near Ryandel, a small town in the southeast corner of BC. This was always one of our

favourite trips. It was easy miles as we travelled south
through Alberta, which was flat and fast, and the BC part
of the trip was short but sweet.

The best part was that we always ran empty from the
mine into Vancouver. This was almost 500 miles, and
although Highway 3 westbound had more curves than a
chorus girls' convention, with no load on we could make
good time. On top of this, there was a small, government-
run ferry operating from the top of Kootenay Lake, near
Ryandel, to (if memory serves) a point at the other end of
the lake, near Castlegar. It was a slow ride and took about
an hour and a half, but it saved almost five hours of having to drive all the way around the lake. Trouble was, this
ferry only ran in daylight hours, so the delay at our
Edmonton office was causing us some concern.

True to their word, the mechanics did their thing,
and we were gone, running about four hours late. Not
wanting to miss that last ferry the next day, we drove like
bats out of hell, skipping coffee breaks and pushing our
bladders to the limit. The road gods were with us, though,
and we arrived at the mine in plenty of time to catch the
last ferry.

We ran into the receiver's office with our bills,
expecting their usual quick unloading service, but we got
a nasty surprise. The receiver took one look at the packing
slip and said, "Boys, you got the wrong size balls. We can't
use these."

Good grief!

Dale quickly called our Edmonton dispatcher and explained the problem. Luckily, it wasn't our screw-up; the mill in Edmonton had got it wrong. After an hour of phone calls, we were instructed to haul the load to Vancouver. The steel mill would handle the problem from there.

Oh, lovely.

That meant we had to forego the ferry ride, make the trip around the lake, and drag those bloody balls over a road that had more twists and curves than a car salesman's contract.

"We can still take the ferry," Dale said as we got back in the truck. "They can handle two loaded trucks at a time, as long as there's no cars. Let's give it a shot."

I was a bit dubious, but what the heck. As we pulled up to the ferry toll booth, we could see there were lots of cars and one truck already on the ferry. There appeared to be room for us, but just barely. Professor Dale decided if we lied about our weight, they might let us on.

Now this sounded a little dangerous to me, because that ferry was no freighter and already looked pretty full. Besides that, Dale was a born-and-raised Prairie boy, and his boating experience was limited to watching soap float in the tub. But he was the boss, and I figured the old senior citizen in that booth would call baloney anyway, so I kept my mouth shut.

I must admit the load we had on didn't look like much. Those steel grinding balls were loaded in old forty-five-gallon drums for easy handling at the mine. They weighed a ton each, and we had twenty-two of them, which was a legal load for the day. This meant there were eleven drums grouped at the very front end, over the drive wheels, and the other eleven grouped over the tandem trailer axles. The balance of the trailer was bare.

Dale pulled up to the toll booth and said, "We gross about 55,000 pounds. These drums weigh 1000 pounds each, and the truck weighs 33,000 pounds."

Be damned if Dale didn't hand over the money and we got our pass onto the ferry. Things were definitely looking up, until we started pulling onto the boat. I remembered from previous trips the two trucks allowed were always placed in the middle of the ferry, with cars ahead and behind, half a dozen at most. The lane we were being directed into already had cars up front, which would leave us on the tail end.

Well, we crept onto the ferry, and as we approached the back end of the car ahead, the lake we could see through the windshield started to disappear. The deck hand who had been guiding us on frantically waved his arms in the air, then covered his eyes with his hands.

A quick look in our mirrors told the story. The ramp we had just come off was now hanging three feet above the deck of the ferry. Everybody knows there is no tide in a lake, so there was only one explanation—this ferry was tilted!

Lucky for us all, there were two large cables securing the ferry to the dock, one from each back corner. They were now stretched like guitar strings, but they appeared to be holding.

"Well, done, Dale," I said. "You've just killed us all."

About this time, another deck hand came running towards us. We assumed he was the captain because he had handles on his shirt and this nifty yachter's cap, although the jeans and deck shoes sort of threw us off. He was a little miffed, to say the least.

"Show me your f——ing bills," he screamed.

Dale handed them over, looking stunned. One quick look and the captain knew damn well what had happened. A short conversation through a hand-held walkie-talkie he was holding convicted us.

The Admiral said, "You got 44,000 pounds on there, not 22,000."

"Oh, for Heaven's sake," said Dale. "What was I thinking? There's 2,000 pounds in a ton. Boy, am I dumb!"

"Yep," I muttered to myself.

I'm sure this was not the first time this had happened to the ferry, as twenty minutes later, two very large D-8 winch-equipped Cats backed up to the dock's edge. Apparently there was a construction company nearby to supply these things. In a very few minutes, they had winched the deck back, level with the ramp. And without hesitating at all, Dale backed quickly off the ferry.

There was no damage done, and the only screaming was who would pay for the crawlers. A couple more phone calls, and that was settled.

But this little episode had not only tacked on five hours to the trip, to get around the lake, but we'd lost two more hours on that stupid ferry. After nearly causing a marine disaster, the balance of the trip was ho-hum. Suffice to say, that was my last trip to Ryandel.

Payback Time

FORGIVE ME FOR dredging up bad memories, but did you ever drive team with a practical joker? Oh brother, I sure did, and I believe I had the grand-daddy of them all.

But I got even.

Now don't get me wrong. Sparky was one of my heroes. As a matter of fact, he was the first company high-miler to accept me when I graduated to long haul. When the going was tough, which was most of the time, winding through the passes in the Rocky Mountains, he was all business. I swear the guy had built-in radar because even in the worst blizzards he always seemed to know where we were and when the next corner or hill was coming up.

Hell, he used to talk to that truck, and I swear it answered him back. On occasion I would hear him whisper, "Whaddya think, old girl? Do you need the chains? No? Okay, let's keep going!" The guy saved our worthless necks a dozen times and he was a great teacher to boot.

But when he had some time on his hands, it was a whole new story. I lost track of the times he would straighten out a coat hanger he'd smuggled into the bunk, slip it through the curtains behind me, hook the air horn chain, and give it a short blast. This never failed to lift me out of the driver's seat, and you could feel the truck rocking from him laying in the bunk, laughing his head off.

You cabover drivers out there will remember the pedestal-mounted transmission sticks that could be removed in order to jack up the cab. One of Sparky's favourite stunts was to reach through the bottom of the curtain, half-way up a hill, and pull the stick off the auxiliary trans. Of course, I never learned to look down to make sure both sticks were in place (these rigs had four-and-four trannies back then), so when I grabbed for the stick to shift down a notch or two, my right hand would be frantically waving in the air, trying to find the missing lever. Of course, this meant having to take a full gear every time I shifted, instead of a handful of little ones. I would let out a string of four-letter words, and the missing stick would silently appear where it should have been all along.

Truckstop restaurants were Sparky's favourites. Would you believe, this guy carried common knives and forks, found in any restaurant, with old gravy or egg stains on them? He would order a meal, and just after the waitress had set down his plate, Sparky would switch silverware, then holler out loud about the condition of his knife and fork, which of course were filthy. He either got a free meal or an escort out of the restaurant, depending on how goofy the staff was. Talk about embarrassing!

His other favourite stunt was waiting for the waitress to say, "What can I do for you?" He would seriously reply, "Burn two pieces of toast, then put your hair in curlers and nag me a bit. I'm feeling homesick." It usually got him a snicker.

Now you can just picture, that since I was the brunt of most of his stunts, I couldn't wait for payback time. Well, that time did finally arrive. Our address for this week or so was COE-KW-Unit 16 and we were headed south after unloading and reloading at a God-forsaken place called Endako in northern BC. We were on our way to Vancouver with a flat deck load of "molly" and all was going well. We were about ten minutes away from our next switch point at a truckstop in Quesnel, which was none too soon, as I was getting tired and hungry. I was half-way up the last hill we had to climb when Sparky bails out of the bunk and says, "Stop the truck! I have to crap."

"Sparky," I says, "we're only ten minutes from the truckstop. Clamp those cheeks and I'll have you there in a jiffy."

"Pull over now!" he says. "I can't wait."

Well, he was the boss, so I crowded the guard rail and came to a stop. He grabbed our emergency roll of paper and out the door he went. I figured no big deal; it was the middle of the night and pitch black.

Just then, a Greyhound bus broke over the crest of the hill and was slowly approaching us.

Lordy, it was payback time!

I released the brakes and let the rig roll back far enough so my headlights were on Mr. Practical Joker. There he was, sitting on the rail, with his shorts around his ankles, and the roll of paper in one hand.

The bus driver gave a mighty toot on his air horn and a big wave. Half a dozen passengers also blew him a kiss.

Look out! In a split second, Sparky was on his feet and running for the rig. I figured I was as good as dead, so I crammed the truck in gear and started climbing. Sparky did a Tarzan-type leap, grabbed the ladder on the ditch side of the truck, and climbed in the cab. Boy, was he hot! It's a good thing for me he only weighed 120 pounds, even with his boots full of rocks, so physical abuse was out of the question.

I was laughing even though Sparky was screaming at me. When he stopped to catch his breath, I said, "See? I knew you could wait for ten minutes!" Oh boy, was THAT the wrong thing to say.

We arrived at the truck stop minutes later and he disappeared into the Men's. He finally joined me in the booth and there wasn't a toot out of him. He didn't calm down until the next morning, and it was only because I told him it was payback time that he finally saw the error of his ways. You know something? There was a whole lot less practical joking after this episode.

I needed the break.

Gone With the Wind

AH, YES, THE wind. Now there's a subject near and dear to us all.

You've got your gentle breezes, but that's poet country. Then there's your Nor'easters and Force-Five blows, but that's sailor stuff. What my fellow gear grinders and I encounter falls into three simple categories: head wind, tail wind and of course, the wind that compressors need. This last one anchors our beast and runs the air-powered do-dads. No sense yapping about that because it's just another accessory until the stupid thing quits.

The other two affect us, big time—right guys? I suppose it's no big deal if you're pulling a deck or tank, but if you're hooked to a ragtop, hi-cube box or a tarped load stacked to max height, that freaking wind can make or break the run. If Mrs. Nature provides a tail wind, that breeze blowing up your kilt saves fuel, gains a couple notches in the tranny and allows you to snicker at the poor schnook going the other direction.

It's the first one—the gerstunkin head wind that causes four-letter words. That sucker can blow holes in your fuel consumption, your schedule and your tarps. I suppose it can happen anywhere, but there are some places in North America where it blows like forty bastards all the time.

Every high-miler you talk to will list off a half-dozen places he's had to grind through and I sure have my own dreaded stretches. Of course, I had it real tough (where have you heard that before?) because the Alberta-based company I drove for ran cabover tractors and a lot of rag-top bullpens.

Mother! There were times when it was faster to get out and walk. I'm sure the names Fort McLeod and the Crow's Nest Pass shoot fear into those other poor souls who, like me, have trucked into southwestern Alberta.

I kid you not, the wind coming out of that mountain pass blows hard enough on occasion to roll a rig right off the road. The Queen's constables used to close the highway sometimes because it blew so bad. Not only were the few trees around all bent in one direction, but I swear the local folks had a permanent lean.

The only funny side of heading into that draft was watching the four wheelers pull out to pass and having to face the head wind and the turbulence my rig was whipping up. Jeez! They'd get up alongside, diddle all over the road, then fall back behind. Thankfully, that breezy stretch only lasted a couple of hours, but on some trips it seemed like days.

We also trucked a fair amount of lumber out of BC, most of which had to be tarped. That was already a pain in the pedestal, but if you had random length boards, it was a horror show. The wind could get into the gaps under your tarp and flap it to shreds. It took hours to tarp it tight.

One of our drivers, nicknamed Don Juan (he had girlfriends at most truck stops and every terminal and for a small fee he would share his friends with us), was a little on the lazy side and found a way to solve the tarping problem. He would just load and go, not bothering to cover it. A few miles short of his destination, he would stop and dig out an old, shredded piece of plastic tarp, about ten feet square, and tack it to the front of his lumber load. He'd pull up to the receiver's yard, bail out of his truck, cursing like crazy and pointing to this crummy piece of tarp.

"That's all that's left!" he'd scream. "Blankety-blank wind storm! I'll have to pay for those tarps out of my own pocket."

Well, nine times out of ten, the customer would feel sorry for him and accept the wet, dirty lumber with no problem. Don would wrap up his piece of tarp and explain he'd have to show it to the owner. He finally got nabbed when he tried this trick a second time on some guy in Calgary. Needless to say, when the boss found out, old Donny was gone like a bowl of prunes in a rest home.

I never thought of the wind being life threatening until I got into a bizarre position in another super-windy spot. It was a standard winter night in the Rogers Pass, with the snow falling and the wind howling, creating a near-whiteout. Every once in awhile I'd meet another rig going the other way and we'd face total whiteout for a few seconds until things settled down. This included getting the rubber back into the ruts in the ice and snow.

Well, I figured things couldn't get any worse until I approached the west gate where the toll booth took your money before your proceeded to the summit. There were already a dozen rigs lined up at the closed gate and the big road condition sign was flashing "Slide Delay." A conversation with the parks guys and a few drivers indicated a four-to-six hour wait, which just wouldn't do. I had figured on a meal at the summit, so hunger was already setting in.

The only alternative was to head back a few miles to the town of Revelstoke, but turning around was out of the question, and westbound traffic was now non-existent. An older Volkswagen Beetle with two young guys in it was also stuck in line, so I promoted a ride back to a restaurant. My second driver preferred a few hours' motionless sleep, so he agreed to babysit the rig.

I squeezed my way into the back of Hitler's Revenge and away we went. Minutes down the road, one guy nudges the other, and jerks head and thumb in my direction.

"Hey! We finally have one of those blankety-blank truckers in our car."

Oh, joy! I wondered what I'd got myself into. The guy seemed almost serious. Did he really hate truckers?

Just about this time, we met an eastbound rig just flying through the storm. As he blew by, that Beetle went right sideways and the blowing snow felt like someone had thrown a white sheet over the whole car. I thought my time had come, but the driver wrestled that little pecker of a car back into his lane. After the colour came back into his hands and cheeks, he started yelling.

"You see? You see? This happens every time we meet one of you clowns. Do you always have to drive a million miles an hour?"

Oh, Jim-dandy. First I figured I was gone with the wind, and now it appeared these two nervous Nellies were going to beat on me. They didn't, though, and thankfully, we got to Revelstoke with no further problems. It cost me two suppers and some jangled nerves, but we got back to the gate at Rogers Pass safely.

I couldn't wait to get back in that big, old truck. Don't tell those two guys, but I never slowed down at all, even after all their raving.

Next to some of those brutal breezes that rip across the Canadian Prairies, that Rogers Pass had to take the cake. The guys who manufacture these trucks for us have done wonders to combat the breeze in the last few years, what with needle-nose cabs, spoilers, top and sides, plus fat increases in fuel efficient power. But the wind continues to be a headache.

Well, that's enough ranting for one day, although a thought just crossed my feeble mind. If every trip was a winner, and our job was easy, everyone would want to drive truck.

Oops.

Come on wind!

The Short Cut

WHAT IS IT with kids and big trucks? The rigs always seem to fascinate them. Any gear grinder will tell you that if you drive by a group of kids anywhere in North America, hands will pop up and pump the air, requesting a few toots on your seven-mile horn. If you give them a short blast, you're rewarded with ecstatic shouts and waving.

If you happen to be parked somewhere, kids will come out of the woodwork, asking where you've been, where you're going, and "can we look inside the truck?" Allowing them a glance inside and a chance to pull the air horn makes you king for the day.

This may not sound like any big deal, but how often do you see a lawyer standing on the street with kids around him, asking about his latest lawsuit?

This story is about one of those truck-loving kids.

Actually, the little dude was a relative named Andy, on the wife's side. It was the 1970s, and I was hauling sticks out of Quesnel, BC. Andy lived with his folks in 100 Mile House, two hours to the south. I met the little guy on one of our first visits to make nice with the relatives. He was eight or nine years old, fairly big for his age, and a real loner.

The kid never said much to anyone, including me. Through the day the fact that I drove a logging truck came up, and little Andy brightened visibly. In his own quiet way, he asked if he could have a ride some day.

Well, we all know that in the trucking game, passengers are frowned upon by owners and insurance companies alike. Passengers were also not real popular with the drivers, as the work could be a little dangerous. I made some vague promise to consider the idea, and left it at that.

In the latter part of June, when school was about to be let out, I got a phone call from his mother. She said Andy had been talking steady about riding a truck and asked if there was any way I could oblige. Well, I hooed and hawed but finally agreed to a trip when he got out of school. She was happy, and Andy was happy. I was still a little dubious.

After a bit of thought, however, I figured what the heck? It was summertime, and the roads were passable. We were hauling less weight because they were softer, and because the constabulary was getting smarter. Also, we had been hauling from the same general area for some time, so there would likely be no surprises.

The fatal day arrived, and Andy was delivered to a pre-arranged pick-up spot by his mother. In the little dude gets, looking proud as hell. I had picked him up on my way to dumping my first load, and to my surprise, my boss was waiting for me at the mill. I figured that'd be the end of my tour-guiding service, but would you believe he didn't say zilch about the kid being with me? He just handed me a map and spoke the dreaded words, "custom cut."

Now, these two words sent shivers down every driver's back. They meant that some rancher had decided to clear a bit of his land and had arranged for a mill to buy the wood. The mill arranged loggers and the trucks for him. Usually this meant soft roads that stretched forever, a million miles from nowhere. I guess I looked a little nervous about this because Bill, the boss, said, "No sweat. It's only a couple of hours out of town, behind the Gibraltar Mine. John Karl's crew is up there with machines, so the load should be fast and clean."

Well, after dumping my load, away we went, and hey! This wasn't half bad. We're talking paved road, all except the short bit into the bush. We tooted along, with Andy asking a million questions. He's no longer the quiet loner, and I'm quite enjoying his company. The little dickens sort of reminded me of me at his age.

Well, we follow the map and by some stroke of luck, find the landing. Believe me, with this logging game, locating landings was mostly luck. These loggers didn't believe in signs and they must have assumed we navigated like migrating geese.

At any rate, we got loaded and Wayne, the loader-operator, shut down his machine. Lighting a smoke, he sauntered over to yap while I was wrapping the load. I mentioned to him my dread of going all the way back on the winding road I had come in on. We had appeared to be going the wrong direction for miles before we got to the right road.

"Ha!" says Wayne. "No problem! I know a short cut."

Now, I should have smelled a rat because the pickup truck Wayne drove was pretty hammered up, and it was a four-by-four to boot, but these clues didn't connect for some reason. I took his directions, figuring what the heck? He sees this kid in the cab with me, so he's not going to send me where it might get sticky, right?

Wrong.

On the way out, Andy is all mouth and eyeballs. We'd got that big load of wood on, and the truck is rocking back and forth, and plenty noisy, too. A few miles up the road, we get to a junction that Wayne hadn't mentioned in his "short cut" directions. I stopped and pondered for a minute, then took what I thought might be the right direction.

Well, we're headed west, alright, but this road is getting awfully narrow, and the downhill grade is getting steeper. I notice that there are no fresh tire tracks on this trail. Not only that, but the last clearing we passed was nowhere near big enough to turn around. Nor was it large enough to be a log landing.

I quickly put two and two together and realized this was not a logging road. Those little clearings were for seismic vehicles or small drilling rigs. We were, however, still on mine property as far as I knew.

Well, as the saying goes, there's no way out but down, so crashing into some pretty low gears, I snaked down the hill. Then I slapped a big, silly grin on my face, and tried to speak calmly.

"Andy, we might hit some bumps, so you better fasten your seat belt." I followed suit, and sure as blazes, two minutes later they came in mighty handy. It seemed that bridges fell into the same category as signs on this road—the mining people never used them.

We hit a creek about fifteen feet wide with about two feet of water running through it. Roaring through that with a mighty splash brought a loud "Yahoo!" from Andy. On the other side, the hill climbed steeply, and now the trees alongside the road were scraping my load.

We came to a steep corner, and all I had going for me was the fact that a logging trailer always follows the track of the tractor pulling it, which beats the tracking action of your standard semi-trailer. Still, how we didn't flip over, I'll never know. Somehow, we kept the rubber side down and the road finally straightened out.

Unfortunately, it was now heading straight down, and my little buddy and I are facing problem Number 2000. We're talking tandem tractor and tandem trailer, with only so many brakes, all of which are rapidly heating up. Logging trucks often carry water tanks for cooling purposes, but we were just a shade short of truly mountainous conditions in the Cariboo.

Hence, no water tanks.

I'd already been gearing up to keep that poor old 350 from exploding, so we were travelling at a fairly good clip. I glanced in the mirror and saw the first wisp of telltale smoke coming out the back end of the trailer. The first thing that crossed my mind was that if Andy and I got killed, his mother would never talk to me again!

Just before my miserable life flashed before my eyes, we broke out of that jungle, smoking and roaring, and into a huge, open area right alongside the highway.

I took one quick look up the road and flew onto the pavement. I looked over at Andy, and he was just beaming. The fearless little dude didn't even know we'd been in trouble. That was just lovely for him, of course. All I could think about was discussing this shortcut with Wayne, so I could impress upon him how close I'd come to wrecking my Fruit of the Looms.

I had to keep moving a bit longer to cool those brakes, but as soon as I thought it safe, I pulled into an open spot and gave my legs a few minutes to quit shaking. Then, taking a quick walk around the rig to check for damage, I gave the front fender a little kiss before I climbed back inside.

On the way into town, Andy asked if we were going back for another load. I bit my tongue and told him that we'd probably had enough excitement for one day.

You know something? That kid was twenty-two years old before I told him how close we'd come to dying. Another mile or so of a grade like that and there'd have been no stopping that truck.

Even as an adult, Andy was impressed.

PART FOUR

WEIRD DESTINATIONS

Rip-Rap Follies

EVER GET THE feeling that the trip's going to be a bummer before you even get started?

Well, that's the way I felt about this one. It was a hot July day back in the mid-60s, and I was at the Edmonton terminal getting my travel orders. The first ominous news I got was about being given a new driving partner. My regular guy had booked off all of a sudden. Uh-oh.

The second queasy bit was my destination. I had a load of steel grinding balls for a new mine in the British Columbia Kootenay Mountains, called Giant Soo. The bad news here was that, for some stupid reason, all mines seem to be placed at the tops of mountains, some of them in pretty rough country. The company I drove for delivered steel products to most of the mines in western Canada, and I'd been to most of them. I didn't know this one, but I could guess. On top of all this, the delivery instructions were pretty vague.

On a good note, the new driver I had been given turned out to be a middle-aged guy named Bill Proach, who had a million years experience. He was a nice guy and a bitch truck driver, too. Just as well.

We were told to head for Wasa Junction, an unpopulated area about fifty miles from the nearest town. We were to pull into a clearing off the road there and wait for the mine crew to unload us. Those grinding balls, about the size of tennis balls, were loaded in forty-five gallon drums weighing about one ton each. You needed a crane to lift them off.

Well, we arrived at our destination midway through the next morning, after an uneventful trip. Only there was no greeting party. All we found was a small freight dock and a sign. No buildings, no crane, no crew, no nothing. So we waited.

We'd been sitting there for the better part of three hours, and we were starting to get a bit anxious. We were also starting to fry on that hot summer day because my 1962 Kenworth cabover didn't come with such luxuries as air-conditioning. No CB radio, either, and certainly not a cell phone. That clearing turned into a boiler, and we only had a few cans of pop to replace the sweat.

Bill and I started talking about an alternate plan. We could see the road that obviously led to the mine disappear into the trees a short distance away. Considering there was no crane or anything else where we were, we figured the instructions must be wrong, so we decided to head to the mine.

How bad could the road be? When they constructed the mine, they must have had trucks go up there. We had to consider good old Unit 21 and its 245-inch wheel base, thanks to the existing BC bridge laws, which made it long and awkward. And with its puny 250-horse Cummins engine, it sure as hell wasn't an off-road truck. The only thing we had in our favour was our short, thirty-six-foot, flatdeck trailer.

Our only alternative was to drop the trailer in the clearing and bobtail to a phone, but that would take forever, and we were being paid by the mile. We wouldn't get a penny for all that pooping around.

So Bill got behind the wheel and off we went, up that dark path. The road was gravelled, and at first the grade wasn't all that bad, so we both figured we'd done the right thing. A couple of things nagged at us, though. This was only a single-lane road, for one, and the mountains around here were high. You could still see snow on top of them.

The road got steeper and windier, and we were down in some pretty low gears to keep from cooking the old girl. We climbed and wound through those trees for an hour and a half, then suddenly broke into the open. We were getting above the tree line, and this stinking trail was now clinging to the outside edge of the mountain. I looked out the ditch-side window and, I swear, I couldn't see the bottom. God knows how high we were.

A few more minutes up this trail and we came to a "rip-rap" turn to the right. Basically, a rip-rap is logs laid and braced in a rock crevice to make up a portion of the curve as a cost-saver, so the road builder doesn't have to blast so much rock to widen the road. Luckily, the hill leveled off a bit at this point, and Bill came to a stop. We both sat there, staring at that corner. There was sure as hell no way to turn around, and we hadn't seen a wide spot since we left the clearing, hours ago.

Out we get, and we walk around on this bridge, mumbling and measuring. Finally it's decided that if we run the left steering tire along the rock, we might swing wide enough to get that trailer around the corner. Well, Bill gets back in the truck, and I stay on the bridge to guide him. He backs up a bit and crams as tight to the mountain as he can, and then starts around the corner.

The tractor makes it across with no problem, and we weren't worried about the weight of the rig because this bridge was well-built. It was the turning span of the trailer that made us sweat. The trailer starts onto the bridge, but by now the tractor is turning very sharply to the right, and the trailer wheels start heading for the edge.

At the half-way point, the outside duals are hanging in the air.

I cover my eyes with one hand and wave like hell with the other to get Bill moving quickly. There's a creak and a groan from that old bridge. I can't look. But Bill's inching it forward and the trailer finally arrives on solid ground again.

Bill stops, steps out of the truck, sits down on a boulder, and lights a smoke. We both sit there, not speaking, for ten minutes; then Bill finally says, "They sure must have used small trucks to haul this mine up here."

Well, there's no way but up, so away we go. We hit two more rip-raps and a lot steeper hills, but by mid-afternoon we figure we can go anywhere.

Just about the time we figure this is somebody's idea of a big joke, we pull into an area that looks like the small crater of a volcano. There's snow everywhere, and right in the middle of it is the Giant Soo mine. Parked just a few feet away is a big-mother of an off-road bed truck, with a large cherry picker crane mounted on it. It dawns on us that's what they hauled all the machinery up here with, and that's what was supposed to come down and pick up our load. It was sure as hell capable of carrying what we had on.

We no sooner stop than a half dozen hard-hatted miners come running over. One guy with "Supervisor" written on his hard hat asked, "How the hell did you get that thing up here, and what are you doing here today? We were supposed to meet you at the bottom tomorrow morning."

"It seemed like a nice day for a drive, so we figured we'd come up to see you," Bill replied with a straight face.

"We're both starved," I chimed in. "We haven't eaten for ten hours, and I'd kill for a sandwich."

The supervisor started screaming orders. He pointed to the cook shack and told us to go and eat as much as we could hold, while four other men were ordered to unchain our load and get it off the trailer.

By the time we got back to our rig, it was empty and all our equipment was hung properly on the headache rack. I asked the foreman why they hadn't put a decent road in, and he explained it was a short-life mine. They only expected to be there two or three years, and it was a small operation.

I then asked if he might have contact with the outside world. He did indeed, and let me use the radio phone they had rigged up. I immediately phoned our dispatcher and asked him if he had any messages for God because we were within a few feet of heaven. After explaining the screw up, I received further orders to proceed empty to Vancouver—if we made it down the hill alive.

Gravity was on our side on the way down, and we still had enough sunlight left in the day to make it beyond the rip-raps, so away we went. Needless to say, we made it back alive, but there were lots of tense moments on the way down. Lots of skidding, swearing and bouncing over rocks the size of basketballs.

We never had to go back to Giant Soo. Maybe they eventually decided to fly the bloody balls in.

Surprise!

MY SECOND DRIVER, Dale, and I had just finished unloading at the Craigmont Mine near Merritt, in central BC. It was a load of steel grinding balls that we had hauled from the mill in Edmonton. It was just before dark on a June evening in 1964, and the trip had been uneventful.

I called the dispatcher from the mine for further orders and things started going downhill. He told me to drop my flatdeck there and bobtail to Kelowna, about six hours away, for arrival 8:00 AM next morning. He said two of our trailers were waiting at the piggyback yard there for delivery nearby. Somebody would be waiting to instruct us.

Now, I'm not saying dispatchers lie a lot, but when they withhold certain important points, like destinations, it spells doom. Ours was not to question why, so away we went.

We pulled into the Kelowna piggyback yard right on time. Still sitting up on the railcars was a single-drop, lowbed trailer with a well-used and very large International Harvester bulldozer sitting on it, along with a flat deck trailer with a push-blade, ripper and canopy. I looked over at Dale and said, "Surprise!"

"Oh goody!" Dale said. "I love surprises."

Also standing there was a whole bouquet of big shots. We discovered that two of them had bought the machine from the other two. The first bad news came from the obvious leader of this group, who claimed he had a great plan.

"The mine where this dozer goes has no machinery to put the crawler together," he said with a proud gleam in his eye, "so we hired a machine shop here in town to attach all the pieces before we make the trip."

"I hate to wreck your day," I said, "but that crawler looks pretty heavy, and this truck of ours only has a 250-horse engine. It's only built for the highway."

Mr. Big quickly replied, "It's only a short trip, about thirty miles out of Summerland, and the hills aren't that steep."

"We only get paid by the mile, and we wouldn't get a penny for screwing around all day here in town."

"We'll make it worth your while," he said with a fatherly smile. "Besides, if you do hit a hill you can't climb, we'll just walk the dozer off your truck and then walk it the rest of the way up to the mine."

Defeated, Dale and I just shrugged.

Minutes later, a crane, a crew and all the necessary tools to reassemble the crawler showed up. We got hooked up to the low bed trailer, with a little banging and swearing, and we pulled it off the railcar, but the crew had trouble making some of the pieces fit, and it took all day to ready the machine. We all agreed it would be foolish to try moving in the dark, so we grudgingly took the hotel room that the brass paid for. Over supper with these guys, I mentioned making this worth our while.

"I'm going to make you rich," said Mr. Big.

He wrote a note on the back of one of his business cards and said, "I'm selling shares in the Ida Mine that we're developing to you drivers for ten cents each. I suggest you mortgage your homes and buy as much as you can, because this thing will be huge."

Well, like old Dale would say, if trips around the world cost five cents, we couldn't afford to get out of sight. Neither of us owned homes or much else, for that matter. So I pocketed the card and thanked him very much. I figured we had to take the good with the bad.

These four big spenders decided to go ahead to the mine site right after supper. We were to start out at daybreak, and they would meet us along the road somewhere.

As planned, we were rolling just before sun-up, and we arrived at Summerland—about fifteen miles up the road—in good time. We took the turnoff marked by an

Ida Mine sign and headed up a gravel road. The grade wasn't all that bad, the road was in pretty good shape, and we were driving right through flowering apple trees, which was kind of pretty. All seemed well.

Four or five miles in, we turned a corner and were staring at a hill that appeared to go straight up, I swear, and ended at the top of some trees. Trouble. We looked hard, but we had no choice but to keep going, so I put the old four-and-four transmissions in the lowest gears available and started climbing.

We got about half-way up and the old girl pooped out. I jammed the clutch in a split second before the engine quit, and back down the hill we went. The brakes on that donut-tired, single-drop lowbed were no raving hell, and the loose gravel on the hill sealed our fate. There was no way we were going to stay in a straight line back to the bottom of the hill, so I gave the wheel a short crank and ran the trailer into the ditch. Praise Allah, we stopped.

There was no sign of the four big spenders, or anybody else, so after a short conversation between ourselves, we decided there was only one way out of this mess. That beat up old bulldozer had to come off.

Well, Dale prided himself on being a bit of a skinner, so he jumped on the dozer and fired it up. Dozer, trailer and all were sitting on a pretty fair sideways slant, and the chances of the machine coming off the back end clean were slim.

I carefully undid the chains, then waved to Dale from a good, safe distance. Poor old Dale was shaking like a leaf, but he shoved the machine into gear and yanked on the clutch. The stupid thing came off the side, but Dale just kept going.

To our amazement, the one track left on the trailer finally reached the rear end and plunked down onto the ground. But our problems weren't over yet because by now, old Dale was frozen with fear and didn't stop.

Good Lord! He was knocking apple trees down like bowling pins!

When he stopped he was right overtop a buried natural gas line that had signs marking it, but when he finally stepped down, he looked proud as punch. To hear him tell it, he wasn't scared at all, but when I pointed out the broken trees and the gas line, he dropped the conversation.

We walked the crawler back up to the tail end of the trailer, gave the rig a little nudge and we were mobile again. The agreement had been to take the crawler as far as we could and leave it. With all the death and destruction around the machine, it was pretty obvious that was what we had done, so we headed back to Kelowna. Even after all the time it took to locate a ramp and deck the two trailers together, which we would haul to Vancouver, there was no further sign of the Four Brothers Big.

But wait, that's not the end of the story.

Two years later, I was in the company of our president and a friend of his who was very active in the mining business. The conversation inevitably turned to mining, and I asked the two of them if they'd ever heard of Ida Mines. Mildly curious, I had periodically checked the financial pages but had never seen it listed. I related that the big spender would have sold me the stock at ten cents. Then there was an awesome silence as both men stared at me, then at each other.

"We do know about Ida Mines," the friend said. "They changed the name before it went on the market. They called it Brenda, and the stock opened at eighteen dollars a share! Did you keep that business card you mentioned?"

"Good grief, no! I tossed it because, after we had to leave that guy's dozer half-way up that hill, I figured he'd never speak to me again anyway, and that beat up old crawler indicated he didn't have much."

All three of us just sat there, shaking our heads.

I guess God never meant for me to be rich.

Doctor Who

YOU'VE GOT TO admit, when we hear words like "crazy," "twisted," "mentally challenged," or "psycho," we sometimes conjure up a certain old-fashioned image. It could be some wild-eyed dude, sneaking through an old house and wailing an axe around. Or maybe it's someone tastefully dressed in a canvas jacket, standing quietly in a room decorated with padded rubber. Well, I'm here to tell you, it's a good thing these old stereotypes are dying out. We now know that there's a whole army of folks out there who aren't firing on all six, but you'd never know it to see them.

Now, I'm not talking about the four-wheelers who insist on sacking your rig no matter how blind the bend is or how many lines are on the road. Nor am I talking about the blankety-blank fellow citizens who squeeze in between your rig and the curb when all your right turn signal lights the length of the rig are flashing like a Las Vegas strip sign. For these people it's a physical problem—no brain at all. Actually, I'm thinking of more unfortunate folks, ones who may have lost their way in life and had the wit to seek genuine professional help. My cap is certainly off to them and to those wonderful medical people who provide them with the assistance they need.

What has this got to do with trucking you ask?

I'm getting around to that.

I called Alberta my home, and I tell you there were more than hockey players and roughnecks living there. One simple observation told me there was a fair sized chunk of the population having trouble coping with life. In our area there were two huge, sprawling mental hospitals that I knew of, each capable of housing thousands. The largest by far was the Provincial Hospital in the town of Ponoka, about eighty miles south of Edmonton in central Alberta. The building and grounds stretched for miles. Now, I was never a guest at this institute— although some say I should have been—but I had a few buddies who worked there, and they told me more than I wanted to know about the place. Actually, the hospital employed hundreds of people, which certainly put Ponoka on the map.

Anyway, I finally got to see the institute for myself and—man!—what a hassle. I was driving for an

Edmonton-based flatdeck outfit, and one of their main commodities was reinforcing steel.

As you may or may not know, anywhere they pour concrete, be it buildings, streets, or whatever, they add these ribbed steel bars for strength. In my day, most of this steel was hauled to contractors' yards, where it was cut and bent into all sorts of weird shapes, then trucked to the construction site. If the project was big enough, the steel contractors would bring in their cutters and benders and prefab these steel bars onsite.

This "rebar," as it's called, is real gravy to haul if it's cut in forty-foot lengths, the same length as our trailers, but at least half of what we trucked was sixty feet long. Picture that this was pretty soft steel, as it had to bend easily. As a result, anything hanging beyond the end of the flat deck dipped like wet spaghetti. This is no prob-lem today, with expanding trailers and wide city streets, but a few years back the city planners hadn't figured on eighty-foot-plus truck lengths. Our only answer then was to add a single-axle pole trailer to the back of a forty-foot deck, which solved the dip problem and allowed us to manoeuver the narrow streets and intersections. Anyone want to check out the turning radius of a trombone when she's stretched out? Forget it.

Another drawback to this nightmare length was backing up. That single-axle sat only fifteen feet from the rear of the semi and had a mind of its own. Every yard we pulled into had to have an exit placed directly ahead of us or a crane capable of lifting the extra trailer onto the deck when we were empty.

Turns out that what we crassly referred to as "Screwy U" in Ponoka was running out of room and was forced to build another huge wing. The project was large enough to warrant prefabbing the rebar right onsite, and I was the lucky guy given the first load they shipped in.

Of course, the loads had to be sixty-footers, so I was blessed with the aforementioned trailers from hell. I also made the mistake of cracking a joke to my dispatcher about driving him to the institute so he could visit his parents, so his directions to the construction site suddenly became vague indeed.

I got to Ponoka mid-day, suffering only one flat tire (bloody bias rubber!) and started watching for signs. The route through town to the—ahem—Cuckoo College was well-marked, but I'd neither heard nor seen any mention of a construction gate. I finally found myself on the main entrance road to the institute, ending up at a parking lot where there was no hope of turning around or backing out.

I'm standing in front of my idling rig, staring across 100 feet of manicured lawn at what is obviously a construction site on the far side, when a man dressed in a white smock walks up to me.

"I'm Doctor Smith," he says. "Can I help you?"

"Not unless you know a way to put this rig over there," I blurted, pointing to the site.

"Well, why don't you just drive it through here?"

He points at the wide expanse of pool-table-like grass.

"Yeah, right!" I fire back with a smirk. "And you wouldn't mind my cutting a couple of canyons into your lawn, right?"

"I wouldn't mind," he says, "and besides, there'll be a lot more trucks coming, I would imagine."

Well, hold the phone! Maybe my problem was solved after all. Here was one of the palace big shots giving me permission to wreak havoc on his lawn! Mightily impressed, I quickly walked a short distance over the grass, digging in a heel once in awhile and finding it acceptably hard. With a friendly wave to Doctor Whositz and a roar and snort from my trusty single-axle V-Liner, I was up over the curb and plowing into lawn.

I'd no sooner pulled into the bulldozed clearing on the other side when half a dozen hard hats appeared, all hollering and pointing.

"Relax!" I tell them, springing from my cab. "That doctor over there told me it was okay to cross the lawn. Where the hell are your construction gate signs?"

One of the white hard hats (he had to be the boss—they always wear white hard hats) pointed toward the good doctor.

"He's no blankety-blank doctor! He's a blinkety-blank patient! Look at his pants and slippers!"

Oops. I hadn't paid much attention to these. Besides, how was I supposed to know they let patients wander around outside?

"You're going to pay for that lawn repair," one fellow hollers.

"Bull tweet!" I reply unconvincingly. "You can't blame me. I'll claim insanity! This looks like a nice place to stay."

"You shouldn't have crossed that lawn!"

"Well, how was I to know? And you never bothered to put up your signs. Do you figure I navigate like a freakin' eagle?"

It turns out I had hit on another hazard in hauling rebar. It's one of the first things delivered to a site, besides the gizmo that digs the hole. Rebar is needed for the foundation. Turns out these construction types were only a couple days ahead of me and had had no chance to mark the truck route a couple of miles back.

Well, calm returned to the college with a couple of large staff members escorting Doctor Who back inside and the hard hats mumbling about the restorative powers of a little sod and seed. Hell, they weren't even ready for the steel! The crane hadn't got there yet, so they ended up pulling my rebar off the side with a dozer.

Needless to say, I left there like a spitball out of a

straw and never heard any more about that grass.

Every once in a while, though, I think back and wonder who is crazier—a guy who steals doctors' smocks or a trucker who craters a hundred feet of perfectly good grass?

Maybe you can tell me.

Spring Breakup

SOMEBODY ONCE WROTE a romantic song about "Springtime in the Rockies," but I'll tell you here and now—it wasn't a trucker. For us, spring meant soft roads, road bans, bone-shattering pot holes and washed-out bridges. I've met very few gear-jammers who'd pay much attention to the greening trees or listen to the birdies tweet.

Of course, we all watched for the spring return of the lumbering Winnebego Roadus Hoggus and the multi-coloured, slow-moving Camper Gawkus Aroundus. These were of fundamental interest to us. For us long haulers, though, spring was mostly a pain where your legs meet.

For most truckers, this was the time of the year the rigs were parked and the pay cheques got piddly. There are still lots of stories of how spring breakup affected highway hauling, but I think the biggest problems arose in field trucking; that is, in the oil fields or in logging.

I hauled sticks for a few years in the Cariboo area of Central BC, and the spring breakup problems there were certainly the most interesting I ever saw. Of course, the cold winters up there were ideal for logging. All the roads would freeze harder than a dispatcher's heart, and with a little iceblading by an army of ever-present, road-maintaining graders, the worst of gravel roads became a virtual freeway.

The good thing about winter driving in the Cariboo was that we could max out our loads without worrying about the law. Due to special conditions, we were allowed winter weights, since no amount of pounding could hurt those roads at that time of the year anyway. We didn't even have to worry about cutting the limbs off the logs because the skidders would drag them to the landing by their butt ends, breaking the frozen limbs off as they went.

Man, could we stack on a good load!

Things changed drastically in the spring. One of the major problems was its length. The season could go on as long as three months before the equipment was able to work in the forest again and our trucks were able to use the roads.

This created a major headache for the mills in town. They had to ensure their stockpile would last this length of time, as the roads were impassable with mud, muck and puddles. Brother, the mills were piling logs everywhere! Any vacant lot near town became a temporary storage yard.

Starting in February, the equipment worked basically around the clock, and we would haul as many loads as our red, little eyeballs could stand.

One of the weirdest places used as an extra storage area in Quesnel was the drive-in theatre, affectionately referred to by the locals as the "groan and giggle." The owners would remove the speaker towers when the drive-in closed in the fall, and they'd rent the property to one of the mills in town for log storage. Located on the outskirts of town, it was perfect because it was cleared, gravelled and the car ramps became natural bunks for the logs. On the other hand, it sure looked strange to see the area stacked with acres of logs, half-way up the movie screen!

The dreaded spring melt traditionally started at the end of March, give or take, and this meant trucking in the middle of the night to beat the onset. Although the snow would be melting during the day, and the roads would be getting muddy, they would freeze over at night and we could make a trip or two before it got sloppy by mid-morning.

By this time, we were sharing the road with lowbeds, which were hauling the contractors' skidders and other equipment into town for repairs. This double road action made things a little dicey. Those low bed trailers didn't "deek" around the corners as well as logging equipment did, and they usually didn't have radios, so we were always on the lookout. Sooner or later, we'd get an ominous radio report from one of the log trucks.

"Broke through and buried at mile so-and-so."

This was the universal signal. It indicated that the road had finally got soft and given way, and that would usually be the end of our hauling for the season. We needed those roads when everything dried up in June, so we didn't want to tear them up any more than was necessary.

Most of the log trucks in the area were parked and abandoned until the breakup period ended, but a few of us lucky ones got several hours' work each day, packing partial loads from the storage areas all over town to the mill. It's a little-known fact that lumber mills are set up to cut certain sizes of logs. None of them can cut everything, and so spring breakup was one of the times when mills traded their logs. The plywood mills would take the large logs called "peelers" from each of the mills and trade "pecker poles"—the smaller, skinnier logs—to the stud mills. This way, everybody was happy and some of the mills could keep working.

I was on one of these swap trips to Prince George after midnight once. One of the old hands, Joe Something-or-Other, and I had loaded some peelers at the Quesnel stud mill and were making the two-hour run to the Prince George plywood mill to "re and re" (restack and reload).

We'd timed the trip to arrive at sun-up, so we could

see more clearly where we were going, as the road was new to us. We'd each put on full loads, as there were no scales to cross, and it was still freezing at night. Unfortunately, we had a problem en route, so by the time we hit Prince George, the sun was well up. With Joe in the lead, we pulled off the pavement and headed down a gravel road.

Now don't get me wrong. Icy roads are a way of life in the truck-logging business, but this road looked like a mirror! With the snow melting during the day and freezing up again at night, the roads were always bad this time of the morning, but this one really took the cake.

I slacked off and gripped the wheel, white-knuckled. Old Joe was pulling away from me, but I figured he must be able to see the black ice too. I'm fighting like hell to get slowed down and keep the rig in a straight line in the middle of the road when Joe's lights disappear.

Good grief! I suddenly realize he's started down a hill. Things are looking up for me, however, as I'm almost stopped, with the rubber still on the road. Then I hear a squeaky voice over the radio. Picture that Joe is a two-pack-a-day man and normally talks like coarse sandpaper. But I know it's Joe alright.

"Maymac! Don't come down! Don't come dow . . . ."

End of transmission.

It doesn't take a brain surgeon to figure out that Joe has run into a spot of trouble. Well, for now, he's on his own because, as much as I've got my rig stopped, the dome on this road is causing me a little concern. Slowly but surely, my stupid truck is sliding sideways, toward the passenger-side ditch. I tried "prayer and swear," but to no avail. It just kept on inching off the road.

Finally, it was time to abandon ship, and I stepped out on the running board. I turned the engine off, gave the door a little pat, and bailed off. There was nothing else I could do. The truck slid into the ditch and went over on her side, gentle as you please. I, on the other hand, went sprawling flat on my back, and was probably hurt more than my truck.

Somewhat dazed, I sat up in the middle of the road, just in time to see Joe crawling over the crest of the hill on his hands and knees. Inch by inch, he made his way up to me. I just sat there and waited.

"Boy, sure slippery, ain't it?"

"Yep," I said.

Being macho dudes, we couldn't cry on each other's shoulders, of course. However, I certainly felt like doing just that. No doubt Joe felt the same, but we both managed to maintain our manly cool.

As it turned out, we were less than a mile from the mill. I slid down this skating rink hill and saw Joe's truck lying on its side as I flew past. I knew that if I could get there on foot, the mill guys would willingly supply a dozer and a loader to make things right.

The story has a happy ending. These Kenworths are

built tough, so all I actually suffered was a broken mirror and some dented pride. Joe scratched up a fender and kissed his mirror goodbye as well. Luckily, neither one of us had been hurt, though the final score was definitely "Icy Road, one—Truckers, zero."

I radioed Bill the Boss and after telling him our tale, got the usual understanding reply.

"If it still runs, why are you calling me?"

God, I loved working for that guy!

Heavy Haul Headache

I FIGURE THE best stories are born when the unexpected happens. The common, everyday stuff becomes fleeting memory, but throw a pickle in the pudding and it can lead to a real knee-slapping story.

One of those pickles hit the fan a pile of years ago, and it still triggers a giggle when I relate it to anyone who'll listen. Granted, it happened quite a few years back, but truckin' is truckin', and the only thing different was that I was a lot younger.

Mind you, by the time this little episode happened, I was too old and silly to drive, so the company figured I was management material. I was now a big shot supervisor, and all I got to drive was a half-ton. Actually, it wasn't a half-bad job, as I still got mixed up in all the weird flat deck loads and heavy-haul problems.

You wouldn't believe the crappola good old NIC got

talked into. Other carriers would have the sense to laugh and hang up the phone, but our sales guys would walk into Operations Division grinning as if they'd just found out their girlfriend wasn't pregnant. It was part of my job to figure out how to move the heavy and humongous chunks of whatever they'd come up with, and those sadistic sales dudes committed us to some mighty strange stuff.

To tell you the truth, it wasn't really all that tough because the company had all sorts of exotic lowbeds, dollies, boosters and such, and if need be, they'd build or buy whatever was needed.

About this time, the Alberta oil field was booming, and there was a hell of a demand for all sorts of heavy equipment. Many of those excavators, bulldozers and what-have-you arrived in Canada by ship, through the port of Vancouver, where I was stationed. When these equipment manufacturing and import companies discovered their machines could move by truck instead of by rail, our business went ape.

In fact, a whole raft of fifty-ton-capacity lowbeds with all the extra wheels and new tractors to pull them showed up quicker than the girls at a Shriners' convention. Trouble was, some of the equipment coming in was heavier than our trailers or the law would allow. This meant the machine would have to move in pieces on more than one truck, then be assembled when she got to where she was going. Some of this stuff moved across three provinces, which was not just a hell of a long and expensive ride, but which also involved a mountain of regulations to adhere to. One of these machines, a big mother-bulldozer, to be exact, became a real pain in the old wazoo.

This Japanese-built brute weighed in at 150,000 pounds when it was all put together, so it had to be stripped down and loaded onto two trucks. The factory that shipped it knew this; therefore, it arrived in Vancouver with the crawler stripped down to about 110,000 pounds and all the other pieces—like the blade, ripper and whatever else—piled on as loose pieces.

All you guys with calculators out there have already figured out that the machine was still too heavy to hit the road, but no sweat! We had moved lots of these and getting them legal was a breeze. We would arrange for the necessary permit ahead of time, starting right from the pier the machine came into and ending at the BC-Alberta border.

Granted, we were a shade heavy to start with, but a half-hour trip to our yard was on the way to the freeway heading east. The shipper's service truck would meet us there to strip the belly pans and few pads off tracks to make her legal. These extra pieces would go onto the second truck with all the other pieces.

Slick, eh?

Well, we get a call to move one of these puppies to Edmonton, so we call the weigh scale to arrange the permit, which the driver would pick up on his way out of town, after we'd done the stripping. We headed down to the pier to load. I arrived in my trusty pickup, with Clint, the heavy hauler right behind, complete with his cabover Freightliner and brand new lowbed jeep and booster.

One look at the machine spells trouble. This one has arrived with the ripper and its great, ugly tooth still attached to the machine. There's no doubt about it; we're talking heavy.

A fast call to the dealer adds to the problem. Even if they had a service truck available (which they didn't), they couldn't strip the machine on the waterfront because of union rules, and they had no intention of paying the dock folks a small fortune to do it.

"Haul it to our shop and we'll strip her in a jiffy," the dealer suggests.

A call to our branch manager is no help.

"You figure the trailer will take it?"

"No problem there," I tell him. "If we can get the tractor hooked up after she's loaded, pulling it is no big deal. The problem is, this thing is huge. It'll stick out like a biker in a gay bar."

We finally agree it's only a half hour run to the dealer's shop, and God hates a coward. We walk the mother onto the rig, put the neck back on the lowbed and Clint takes a mighty heave under the neck.

Well, blow me over! He's all hooked up and nothing's busted.

We decide to leave the dozer running because they have to be boosted to start. The batteries are dry during the shipping. Restarting is a real time-consuming headache, and it's coming off in half an hour anyway. Clint's not real happy because we have to go right through downtown Vancouver, and past the police station to boot.

"We're going the wrong direction for the permit," he says.

"Relax!" I tell him. "Who's going to mess with this monster?"

Famous last words.

We head out, looking like a parade, me in the lead with my revolving light on top of the pickup and that brand new, shiny rig with a rumbling crawler filling the floor and hanging over the sides. And we're attracting attention like a pot roast at a Weight Watchers' meeting.

Half-way up the only hill to climb, our day takes a dive. A city policeman comes out of the traffic jam we're creating. He pulls in between us and stops. The officer walks up to Clint's door as I hustle my way back to the rig.

Now, old Clint is built like a bear, fears nothing and is never short of words, but this time, he's just staring out the windshield. He's the colour of milk and he's ignoring the cop. I put on my politician's grin.

"Morning, officer! What's the problem?"

"That machine looks awful heavy," he hollers over the racket of Clint's engines and the ground-shaking rumble from the dozer.

I point to a plywood sign tied to the dozer's grill. The sign names the dealer and shows the letters EDM, which all these machines arrive with in port.

"This machine's heading for Alberta, but she's not heavy yet! We're on our way to the dealer's to get the cab and other stuff put on her."

He stares at it for a sec, then asks for my city permit.

"It's in the pickup," I say.

I rummage through some papers in the glove box. Then I give him a stunned look.

"Aw, shucks! I think I left it on my office desk. We move a lot of this stuff, so we get a yearly permit for the max size and weight." I grinned. "We've got a hell of a traffic jam here!"

Brother, that was no lie!

With Clint having to straddle both lanes, the cars were backed up to the horizon. I give the cop my "helpful" face.

"If you want us to get up to a wider spot, we can make some phone calls and sort this thing out."

The cop looks back at the two solid lines of cars, then stares at me for a sec.

"You can go, but you better have that permit with you next time we meet."

"Guaranteed, officer, and thanks!"

I give Clint a "let's go" wave and watch in my mirror as the front axle of that Freightliner leaps a foot into the air, plonks back onto the road and we're rolling.

Twenty minutes later, we're at the dealer's shop. Clint bales out of the truck, runs up and gives me a rib-cracking hug.

He buys lunch, I quit shaking, and that infernal machine comes off. Actually, we hadn't broken the law, just sort of bent it a bit. We did have the government permit after all, even if it fell a few pounds short.

I crap you not. We never tried that again, and the City of Vancouver police department gained a couple of buddies.

PART FIVE

CRAZY CARGO

Crated Critters

HEY, WE'VE ALL had heroes, right? You know, the ones who always make the right moves. Heck, I've had dozens, but I must admit, a few of the guys who drove for the company in Edmonton that first hired me stood out like gods.

Picture me at nineteen years old, joining up with an established trucking company that went everywhere and did everything. I was as green as a two-week-old tomato, and here were all these old hands, these senior dudes, who could long haul, heavy haul, overhaul—you name it.

These guys were driving the biggest and newest long haul cabovers when the only thing I was allowed to pilot was a single-axle IHC cornhusker 427 with a tandem-axle flatdeck trailer. I could travel a 200-mile radius, which was like driving around the corner for these guys. They were all tough as two-dollar steaks, and they had great nicknames, like Zorro, Chrome Stack, Yabba Dabba, Cat, Sparky, and Little John.

Now these were not your sexy, CB radio handles. Heck, those things weren't invented yet. These were rough, English translations of unpronounceable, Ukrainian names. As a matter of fact, the outfit I drove for was owned and staffed mostly by Ukrainian guys, born and raised in small towns around Alberta. They even tried to teach me some words in their native language, but the first time I tried them out on a Ukrainian waitress, I was escorted out of the cafe. Whew, boy! That had those smart-ass high-milers rolling on the floor.

Unfortunately, I was blessed with the nickname "The Kid," because of my age, and would you believe that sucker stuck on me until I was in my thirties? Anyway, I swore I'd be as good as these old hands were some day, and eventually they allowed me into their circle. Learning from them through the years, I finally arrived at long haul status, but I doubt I ever got as good as they were at trucking.

One great example of what these characters could accomplish is a story about two of them team driving on a particular trip eastbound. Zorro and Little John had reloaded some cast-iron something-or-others in Vancouver for transport to Edmonton. They were heavy pieces and were heaped up, front and back, on a forty-foot flatdeck, leaving twenty feet of empty deck in the middle.

The Grand Poobah of the Vancouver terminal handed them their running orders and two sets of bills. He pointed to one set of these bills, which listed a pickup address in the Fraser Valley on the way out of Vancouver and only stated, "On company service, two crates, 450 pounds."

Zorro found this a little ominous and said, "What's in the crates?"

"Don't know," claimed the Poobah. "You'll find out when you stop to pick them up on your way out of town. It's no big deal; you just haul them to our Edmonton yard."

Well, the boys did as they were told and arrived to pick up the crates at a feed store listed on the bills.

"Finally you're here," said the shipper. "I'll forklift 'em out and set 'em on your trailer."

Out came the first crate, with a live goat inside. Zorro took one look and said, "No way! We don't haul critters."

He got on the phone to the Vancouver boss, who told him, "It's President's orders. It's another one of his stupid favours to a friend."

In the meantime, out came the second crate, identical to the first.

Well, that phone call had sealed the deal. It was haul the goats or quit, so onto the trailer they went.

"You boys realize you'll have to stop every couple

hours to give the girls feed and water," the shipper said, and probably with a straight face. "Not to mention one of them is pregnant and will have to be milked pretty regular."

The guys exploded. Little John hollered, "We've got to quit this outfit if we ever get home!"

Zorro asked wryly, "Which goat was out on the date?"

They shook their heads in disgust, but being old farm boys, they knew what was necessary, so away they went. They very quickly set up a schedule for the zillion stops they would have to make, but half-way along, they changed it. By one of them staying out on the trailer to do the milking duties, etcetera, through the slats of the crate, the other driver could continue slowly on. Thank Buddha it was summertime, so the weather wasn't a factor, only the wind.

Well, lucky me. I happened to be in the Edmonton yard, having just returned from a trip myself, when I saw good old Unit 21 coming along the road toward the office. I did a double take, then broke out laughing, because there was Little John on his hands and knees, with his arms stuck in a crate of some kind, and the wind just ripping at his jacket. I couldn't wait for them to pull up, so I could find out what the hell this was all about.

They both came stomping up to the office, smelling like a barn yard, and mad as hell. They marched past the receptionist straight into the owner's office, with half a dozen of us other drivers following and giggling behind.

The truck keys landed on the boss' desk, and Zorro screamed out, "There's your keys and your critters. We quit!"

Of course, we were all aware these guys got paid by the mile, same as the rest of us, so this particular trip was a big loser.

Well, the owner of the company very seldom smiled, but he had a beauty on at this point. He grabbed his jacket, told the receptionist he and "every truck driver around here" was away for the balance of the day. He knew damn well if he bought the beer for the afternoon, the boys would calm down, and this would make a great story. He also agreed to tack a little extra loot onto their next pay cheques, to cover the babysitting duties. Of course, we all knew that wouldn't amount to much, as the old man was tighter than ten-dollar boots. But it did the trick.

See? Didn't I tell you these guys could do anything? Even those two goats were impressed.

Character Builder

I SWEAR, SOME loads are just plain jinxed before you even back under the trailer. Cursed right from the start. You all know what I'm talking about.

At Northern Industrial Carriers, we hauled everything from soup to nuts. When I showed up at the home terminal in Edmonton, I never knew what the hell I was going to get. It could be a flatdeck load of steel something-or-others, maybe asphalt shingles, or drummed chemicals with weird names and smells. Other terminals were the same, with the freight stretching from "jammy" loads of potato chips or mattresses to some god-awful, oversized machine. The one bad luck load that takes first prize in my mind was fibreboard insulation. It was usually stacked as high as laws would allow and had to be fully tarped. What a hassle.

Well, I got a load of this stuff put together one day, and even on my way back to Edmonton for paperwork and fuel, the trailer lights went out. I knew right there the jinx was in. Hours later, with the trailer repaired, my tanks full, and my fist full of paper, I headed out. This was one of the few trips that I was running single, as my usual second driver and even the spare-board drivers had all disappeared. The trip to Vancouver back then took me south to Calgary and then straight west on the Trans Canada to Vancouver. Naturally, a headwind came up on the outskirts of Edmonton and blew hard enough to peel paint all the way to Calgary. With just 250 horses, it was like trying to drive underwater.

Heading west out of Calgary, I felt a wobble and heard some racket. I checked my ditch-side mirror in time to see an outer wheel leave the trailer, go airborne, and sail into a deep ravine. It was history, and moving so fast I'll bet that baby rolled for a week. Luckily, I was able to creep into a truck stop up the road and slap on the spare I always carried.

Believe it or not, I got to Vancouver with very little else going wrong. I hoped I'd used up the entire curse, but no such luck. The dispatcher ordered me to pull the trailer to its destination at the Park Royal Shopping Centre in North Vancouver and then spot it for unloading. I'd never been in this part of the city, and as he described my best route, the dispatcher mentioned that it included a tunnel. No problem. I hadn't measured it, but I figured the load would be legal height. So away I went.

I started into that tunnel somewhere around 7:30 on Monday morning, with traffic all over the place, naturally. I got a full trailer length inside the tunnel and saw that it ran about three trailer lengths long. Now, it was your usual arch shape, so I wisely went down the middle of the road, staying under the highest point.

I'm taking it pretty easy and staring at the load in the mirror when the tarp starts to creep up the front of the load like a new bride's nightie.

So I jerked to a stop and bailed out to take a peek. Sure as God made green apples, there was either a low spot in the roof or a high spot in the road, as the front end of that load was jammed into the ceiling. I quickly realized the high-mount fifth wheel and the no-give, rubber block suspension on this rig made the load higher at the front.

Well, wouldn't you know, with hundreds of unhappy car drivers around me, the one right behind me was a member of the Queen's finest. He must have been passed over for promotion the day before because he was real cranky.

"You're overheight, blah, blah, blah," he went on. "You should have known better, blah, blah, blah."

I meekly pointed at the back of the trailer, desperately trying to be pleasant.

"It's not the load," I said. "It's your tunnel. Look at the clearance I have at the back end."

That seemed to calm him down a smidge, and he finally said, "Now what do we do?"

Luckily, I knew from past experience there was only one way out of this mess. I opened the fifth wheel, leaving the air lines and light cord hooked up. I slowly pulled ahead and let the trailer drop onto the three feet of frame sticking out behind the fifth wheel. Fortunately, flatdeck carriers always have lots of chains, so I ran a spare one from the base of my headache rack to the front of the trailer and cinched it tight. I now had the clearance to get the rest of the way through that tunnel. It was a good thing the load was light, so backing under the trailer again was no problem. The cop was so impressed with my quick solution—not to mention being faced with ten miles of cars stratching in both directions—that he just gave me a wave and away I went.

Minutes later I arrived at the shopping centre and pulled up at a partially constructed building the size of three football fields. After a half hour of wandering around, I found the roofers who were waiting for this load, and they told me where they wanted it parked. Good grief! It was like an obstacle course inside, but I finally got the trailer backed in, the length of a block inside this monster building. With tarps removed, my equipment all stowed and the bills signed, I figured I'd finally rid myself of that cursed load and trailer.

Fat chance.

I was eastbound later that day with something "jammy" and soon forgot about that jinxed westbound trip. But I was back in Vancouver a week later, and that same heartless dispatcher asked me to bobtail down to Park Royal and pick up the now-empty trailer that I'd spotted there the week before.

I got to the place where I'd left the trailer and—oopsy!—we had a problem. The walls of that building were all up, the roof was half in place, and that stupid trailer was still sitting inside, with no way of getting to it. I figured Eatons might have to buy it and use it for change rooms or something because there was no way to get it out of there.

With a big, cocky grin on my face, I found the roofer and asked him how exactly I was supposed to get my trailer out. He looked quickly around at the walls, the trailer—and then at a big-mother hole in the roof. Without saying "boo," he walked away, putting one hand up to say I should stay put. Twenty minutes later he showed up again, and I looked up through the hole in the roof to see the boom of a big-mother crane swing over the hole.

Luckily, that hole was over top of the trailer, and in ten minutes the riggers had chained the trailer to that monster hook and the trailer disappeared over the roof. Now this was some big deal, because it was a three-storey building. That trailer sure looked weird hanging fifty or so feet in the air, but in no time at all that deck was plopped down just five feet away from my tractor. Other than having to pull the stupid thing out through that obstacle course made up of curbs and construction clutter, I finally rid myself of it at our yard.

They say adversity builds character, but I think it leads to more practical outcomes. That's why we kick the tires, right, guys? We're not checking for flats, we're getting even!

Don't Ask!

THIS LITTLE EPISODE occurred in the late 80s. I now held the lofty position of supervisor at the Vancouver terminal.

It was a decent day in the summer—a Friday, and it was late in the afternoon. All the trucks we had expected for the week had been and gone, and I was hanging around the office, looking forward to getting off work in time for a change. This didn't happen often in the trucking game.

As I waited, a very large, black Lincoln, with two men inside, pulled up in front of the office. I watched with interest, as the two of them talked in the car before getting out. I couldn't help but wonder what they might be after at this time of the day. They finally emerged, each pointing at a row of trailers parked nearby. Then they walked into the office.

I noticed that both wore expensive suits, but to me they looked shifty as hell. The spokesman of the two weighed 300 pounds minimum and spoke with a throat full of gravel. The other guy stood off to the side, in the foyer, and just stared around.

"I want to rent one of your trucks," the big guy said, after I asked if I could help. I put on a friendly smile and explained he was out of luck because the last of the highway trucks had already left for the weekend. I suggested that perhaps I could help him next week.

"I need to ship some stuff from here to Edmonton early tomorrow morning, and it's gotta go," he said.

Again, I apologized, but he wasn't taking no for an answer.

About this time, our local town tractor pulled into the yard with an empty flat deck. As luck would have it, the big guy saw him.

"What about him?" he asked, jerking a thumb.

I explained that this truck was equipped for the highway, but that I depended on him for our local work and needed him here for seven o'clock Monday morning.

Of course, I knew that the driver we had on that truck, good old Earl, would like nothing better than a weekend trip to Alberta. That Peterbilt truck he drove was sleeper-equipped, very dependable, and very fast. Not to mention that Earl could always use the money. To tell you the truth, I wasn't really interested in helping these guys, as we'd had a long, tough week, and I was looking forward to some time off.

"You gotta understand," I told them. "The only way this truck could be back here for Monday is if he came right back, empty from Edmonton. He can't reload for the return trip until Monday, so this deal is out of the question."

The big guy didn't miss a beat. He pulled a huge roll of bills out of his pocket.

"How much if I pay the truck to come back empty?"

"What's the difference?" I replied, trying to keep my eyes from popping. "You haven't even loaded him yet, and that would probably take most of Saturday."

"It'll take twenty minutes to load one of those big, white, enclosed trailers at 6:00 AM tomorrow," he said. "He'll have lots of time."

"The rig would cost three thousand dollars, for the round trip," I replied, figuring he would tell me to forget it, and split. I didn't like the look of these two guys anyway.

Well, good grief! He started peeling bills out of this roll of his. That was when I realized these guys were serious, so I went in to tell the terminal manager about the situation.

"Well," the manager said, "if the guy's willing to pay cash for the rounder, what the hell? What does he want to ship?"

I walked back out and inquired what they wanted to put into the trailer.

"Don't ask," was the response.

My feet became slightly colder than they'd been before.

"Listen, guys. We have to have a document or bill of lading to cover the shipment, as the government scale people may ask to see it. So we need to know what's in the load."

The two guys looked at each other for a few seconds.

"Lawn mowers," the big guy said.

"No lie!" I said, not believing a word. "Unfortunately, it'll take a lot longer than twenty minutes to load a trailer full of lawn mowers."

"Relax!" he said, waving a careless hand. "There's only six boxes."

My jaw dropped.

"You want forty-eight feet of semi-trailer for six lousy boxes?"

No reply.

By now, there was a pile of cash on the counter. I shrugged my shoulders and counted the money.

"You've made a mistake," I said. "There's $3500 here."

The big guy smiled broadly and said, "The extra's for you."

What could I say?

"You got your truck." I called Earl in and told the big guy, "Here's the driver."

The two of them just nodded at Earl and didn't volunteer any names. Like I figured, Earl was all for it, and didn't care what they put in the trailer. They asked him if he knew where the mini-warehouse was on Schoolhouse Road in Coquitlam, about forty-five minutes away. Earl nodded.

"I'll see you there at 6:00 AM," said Mr. Big, making ready to leave.

Before they left, I had to ask one more question. I still had to make up the paperwork, so, like the nice man said, I listed "one truckload lawn mowers."

"I need the name of the company shipping them and the address and name of the place where we take them in Edmonton."

Again these two guys stared at each other. Then Biggie said, "Toro. I don't have any addresses. We'll show the driver where to go, as we're going along with the truck."

With trepidation, I signed this incomplete bill, and when I handed it over to my "customer" for a signature, he passed it to the little guy, who scribbled something on it. I picked out the number of the trailer Earl was to pull, handed him the bills, and told him he was on his own. Then I gave him a gentle warning.

"Earl, you better be on time, or you and I may not see another sundown."

The balance of the story was supplied to me by Earl, as I never saw these guys again. Turns out Earl was at the mini-warehouse right on time, and was directed to a particular door. The two shifty guys, and two other equally shifty characters, lifted six cardboard boxes with "Toro Lawnmower" written on them into the van trailer, closed the doors and put their own padlock on it. No words were spoken, except by the big guy, who merely said to Earl, "Stop when you're hungry." And away they went, with the Lincoln close behind.

With six lousy boxes that weighed practically nothing, Earl could fly. He didn't stop until he got to Kamloops, where he pulled into a truck stop. The two shifties and Earl walked into the coffee shop and Mr. Big ordered steak and eggs for the three of them, without asking who wanted what. He picked up the tab when they had finished, and away they went again. These guys hadn't said five words the whole time.

There were only two other stops all the way to Edmonton, and they arrived at yet another mini-warehouse around 2:00 AM Sunday. Off came the lock, and two more greasers showed up from nowhere. As they unloaded the six boxes, the big guy walked up to Earl, handed him 200 dollars, and gave him a slap on the back. Earl said he thought his shoulder was broken. The big guy was actually smiling.

There was a fairly new and classy hotel a few minutes

away, and Earl was instructed to follow the Lincoln there. Mr. Big said, "I'm getting you a room so you can get a little sleep, because you done a great job."

"I've got my own bunk," protested Earl, but the guy wasn't taking "No" for an answer.

Up to the hotel desk the three of them went, and once again, out came that great wad of cash. The guy peeled off some large bills and said, "Give my man the best room in the house. There's a little extra here to cover breakfast in the morning."

As the two guys were walking out of the lobby, Mr. Big smiled at Earl.

"You better be back in Vancouver for 7:00 AM tomorrow, or that boss of yours will kill you."

And they both laughed like hell.

Earl said it was the creepiest thing he'd ever seen, and he never did discover what was in those cartons he'd hauled.

Goodbye, Balls!

WOULD YOU BELIEVE, that of all the commodities we hauled on our flatdeck trailers, the highest volume product was solid steel balls? Every mine in the world uses them to grind whatever ore they mine, and they come in sizes from golf ball to softball.

The steel mill in Edmonton produced these grinding balls, and for years we hauled them to every mine in BC. All the drivers loved them because they were easy to handle. We had special "bullpen sides" built for our flatdeck trailers. The sides were two feet high and were held in place by steel pins that dropped into pin rackets all the way around the trailer. They were tied together by hooks and rings.

Putting the bullpen together was the only work the drivers really had to do. The steel mill had big-mother magnets and could load these loose balls a ton at a time, so twenty-two passes meant you were loaded. In addition, all the mines were equipped with a downhill ramp, ending at a large bin. It was a simple matter of backing down the ramp and pulling out the tailgate. The grinding balls would unload themselves.

You could go like hell with a load of these, and every once in awhile one of the boys would go a little too fast. You haven't seen anything until you see a load of these things tip! They fly everywhere, like throwing a handful of frozen peas.

This happened to a load late one night, west of McBride, BC. These balls were golf ball size and filled the ditch and surrounding forest. It was springtime, so there was still snow in the ditch. A recovery crew was organized first thing next morning at our Edmonton terminal. In most cases, recovery of these stupid balls calls for a lot of drivers with buckets. This time we sent up eight guys and a winch truck, along with twenty-two empty forty-five-gallon drums, with their tops cut off. The boys would fill their buckets, then empty them into the drums. When the drums were full, the winch truck would lift them onto the deck of a recovery trailer sent up from Edmonton. Theoretically, there should have been twenty-two drums-ful, because each drum held one ton.

After three days and nights of backbreaking work, only eighteen drums had been filled. Robbie, a driver with a great sense of humour, made the bad news phone call from the nearest town to Simon, the company owner. Rob meant to advise him that the job was finished. Simon asked if we had got them all, and Rob had to admit there were only eighteen drums, not twenty-two. Obviously, many of these heavy steel balls must have buried themselves in the surrounding area and couldn't be found, but Simon figured the boys were just being lazy.

"Where's the other four damn drums?" he hollered.

"We think the bears ate them," Rob retorted. "We didn't actually see them do it, but you can hear them crap at night, and it sounds like thunder!"

Even Simon had to laugh.

"Alright, alright!" he said. "Send the eighteen drums to the mine and come on home."

From that day on, any of our drivers who heard thunder rumbling in the sky never passed up the opportunity to joke about it.

"Listen to those bears crap, will you?" they'd say, and those of us who'd been there would burst out laughing all over again.

And the Winner Is . . .

JUST RECENTLY, WITH a little quiet time on my hands, I started thinking (well, having a blond moment, really) about some of the rotten loads I had to truck through the good old days. I know some of you are thinking that's a little negative—that somebody must have bumped my walker and put me in a poor mood—but really, I got quite a kick out of it. I realized that Mr. and Mrs. Public have no idea how much crappola we truck on their behalf every day.

For one thing, they never get to see it because it's sealed up in a high-cube box or some kind of van or stacked on a flat deck, all wrapped up in a heavy mother tarp. I'm not talking about canned goods or other palletized stuff. The forklift puts them in; the forklift takes them out, blah, blah, blah. I mean the raw material stuff.

Let's face it. By the time Joe Average gets a look, it's already bolted in a building or stacked on a store shelf in its finished condition. Well, I picked out a few commodities that I could certainly have lived without and I'll bet other drivers will agree.

How about those gerstunken cow hides! Oh, how we all hated those. I couldn't count how many guys lost their lunch when they opened the van doors on their first load. The smell was worse than a Sumo wrestler's jock strap, and the hides appeared to be moving, they were so full of maggots. I certainly lost a few Big Macs in my day. Mind you, not everyone was a coward around them like I was. Some of the waterfront guys or treating plant crew who unloaded those trailers acted as if they were handling clean sheets. Go figure!

Reloading the trailer with general freight after hauling a load of those puppies was a joke. Most of us just insisted the company throw the trailer away. In order to clean the stupid thing, you'd have to skip two meals, then take a deep breath and run in with a hose. That would take care of the lumps and the last few maggots that figured they had a new home, but it sure didn't help the stink. We'd sprinkle cans of coffee—any brand would do—all over the floor, which would help, but left with the doors closed for a couple of warm days, she'd still double you over the duals when you cracked her open. You see, by the time the public gets a look, they're already shoes and purses. Did I get any thanks for making that possible? Not a sausage!

The next thing on my list of never-agains is plastic-covered steel pipe. When you truck bare steel pipe, rusty and all, it's a piece of cake. Once it's properly in place, it'll stay put until the cows get back from the movie, but look out when they put that protective coat on it. Now, I realize it's necessary because, number one, it's going to be buried in the ground, and without that coat it would last as long as a pickled herring at a Norwegian wedding. Number two, the public needs the natural gas, fuel oil and whatever other juices they blow through it, but does Aunt Mazie care how the gas got to her McLary? Hell no! Just ask any of my fellow pipe stringers out there how careful we are with that stuff and how many times we've seen it stuck through some guy's cab when he had to "heave to" real quick. Actually, it's not all that bad in the summertime, or when it's dry. It's the winter time, when it's frosty or covered in frozen water beads, that it brings the hair up on your neck.

I remember a case where one of our guys, Al Something-or-Other, didn't even make it out of town with a load of those torpedoes. He braked hard at an intersection in Edmonton to miss a red lighter and part of his load shifted ahead. One of the four-inch pipes he was carrying shot through the back window, plucked his cap and some hair off his head and smashed through the windshield. When we got there to clean up, that pipe was sticking eight feet past the front of the hood, with Al's cap still dangling off it!

Al was wandering around nearby, holding a cloth to his head and mumbling something in French (he was from Quebec). Half the load was stuffed into the back of his cab, which came close to putting his lights out, but he seemed more upset about that torn cap. They never talked him into pulling another load of that and I wish they had shown me the same courtesy. To this day, I still lie down on the seat when I hit the brake in my car. No, really!

Another cargo that gave me the willies was drums of chemicals. For one thing, I usually couldn't pronounce the name of what we had loaded and the manufacturer would slap these ominous warning stickers all around the trailer and attach a spill procedure warning on the manifest.

"Oh great," I figured. "If I take one sniff of this stuff I won't be able to have children, or my skin will peel like a grape."

The trip always seemed a lot longer, and out of habit I'd just hold my breath at tire thumping time. There always seemed to be a leaker in the load and the smell would force flies off a cow pie when you opened the doors. Once the fumes hit me, I'd do a quick body inventory to make sure nothing was rotting off. I'll bet that's what stunted my growth. Evil trash!

As bad as these things are, first prize goes to barbed wire. Sheesh! What terrible stuff that is. My worst load of all time started out in Vancouver, where my second driver, Danny, and I were dispatched with a forty-five-foot dry box to a wire company in town. I won't mention the name of it because I can't handle a lawsuit right now. My lawyer is still doing three-to-five for the last case he handled.

Anyway, this company made nails, bedsprings and barbed wire, amongst other things. It was a fairly new plant, but some twisted architect had neglected to put in a loading dock. This meant the forklift would stick the pallets at the tail end and we had to use a hand jack to run them ahead and place the load. No big deal, really.

Turns out, though, there was an agreement with the receivers to pay for or return the empty pallets, and this day no such luck. We discover on arrival to load that the shipment is going to some off-the-beaten-track government job in southern Alberta, and they didn't want pallets. Our day took a dive. This meant we had to unload twenty-two tons of barbed wire off the pallets and floor-stack it.

That stuff comes in two-roll packs, tied together with a bit of a wire handle at the top. A pack weighs about forty pounds and it's covered in those bloody barbs, which means you have to hold them out and away from your legs. One slip and we're talking hamburger.

Realizing that fifteen minutes of whining and snivelling wasn't working, we finally got down to business and hand-flogged that whole load. Three hours later, with torn gloves, shredded jeans, and arms stuck in wing position, we slammed the doors. The bills had a map attached, directing us where to take the wire and we arrived in the middle of nowhere, staring at an old, abandoned military airfield, converted into a World War II prisoner-of-war camp. We'd both seen enough old movies to recognize what we were looking at.

"Jeez!" Danny says. "They must be rebuilding this thing. War must have broken out again!"

We drove through the unlocked gate and went back in time. The fences and buildings were in pretty rough shape, but the camp was huge. We figured the Canadians must have planned on capturing the whole Nazi army.

Minutes after we arrive, a car pulls up with an official-looking senior citizen behind the wheel. He signs the bills I hand him and tells me "stack it over there," pointing to one of the buildings.

"Where's your crew?" I ask.

"Boys, we bought the wire delivered on the ground. You're the crew."

Danny asks if any of the prisoners who are left could give us a hand. The old coot laughs and says he's not sure how many prisoners were actually kept here, but he doubts that any would want to return and help.

"Just pitch them off, boys. You can't hurt the wire and the pile doesn't have to be pretty."

"Is it any of our business why you're re-fencing this place?"

"Yeah. This time we're trying to keep people out.

Hunters and such keep coming around, setting fires. It's still government land, so we have to protect it."

"Why put a camp way out here?" I ask.

"Well," he replies, "the prisoners would travel by train from the coast, and if they saw how far it was inland, they would think escape was impossible."

That made sense, and so, unfortunately, did the fact that Danny and I would have to hand flog that whole load again. Twenty-five years later, my arms still ache, but my legs have healed quite nicely.

Well-known for his joke- and story-telling abilities, DON
MCTAVISH was employed in almost every aspect of the
trucking industry from 1958-1997. Encouraged by
friends and family to document his wacky and funny
trucking experiences, Don McTavish originally found a
place for his stories in the trucking trade magazine
Highway Star where he writes a feature section entitled
"This Ain't No Bull." Born in Calgary, Alberta, Don is
now retired and lives in Vancouver, British Columbia,
with his wife Marg, where he spends his time writing and
staying in touch with his friends and four grandchildren.

Epilogue

TO SAY "THE END" doesn't sound right.

Let's just say we've arrived at our terminal, the rig is parked and the paperwork is done. If you feel that you were along with me on a couple of runs, then the book has fulfilled its purpose. I hope you enjoyed reading these stories as much as I did writing them. I also hope I've stirred up a little curiosity among the younger readers, and that they'll consider a career in truck transport. If they're anything like me, they'll love every minute of it.

Keep the rubber side down!